"What a difference a book can make! Bud Haney and Jim Sirbasku don't tell as much as they show the way to be successful."

BERNARD RAPOPORT
Chairman Emeritus and Founder
American Income Life Insurance Company

* * *

"Passion and Focus! *40 Winning Strategies* is a simple and easy read about 'passion and focus' that will guide you to attain things in business and life that you never thought possible. I am giving this book to everyone that I care about!"

JOE FERTITTA
Vice President Southwest Operations
MGM Mirage Marketing

* * *

"It's hard to think of a problem for which they haven't provided a 'how to' strategy. You'll want this book close at hand."

AIDAN FURLONG
Country Manager
Sun Microsystems

* * *

"A terrific read. I can't think of a better way of planning for the future than reading and re-reading these 40 in-your-face inspirational strategies."

JOHN SAUNDERS
Managing Director
Fleishman-Hillard Saunders

* * *

"This book is perfect. It covers all the essential ground with practical advice in bite-size chunks. It's my desk-top business bible."

WILLIE WALSH
CEO
Aer Lingus

* * *

"Inside this book's pages, as within their office walls, Jim Sirbasku and Bud Haney reveal the brilliance of sales millionaires. Modeling successful selling pros makes you more money. Read about two of the best and make more trips to the bank."

DAN SEIDMAN
SalesAutopsy.com
Speaker and Author of *The Death of 20th Century Selling*

* * *

"Great refresher of good advice for senior managers all in one book—excellent plane reading."

DANUTA GRAY
Chief Executive
O2

* * *

"An important and unique look at self-improvement; Haney and Sirbasku cut to the core of success in business and life. If you want to know how to make a difference and experience life satisfaction, you must read *40 Winning Strategies*."

LARRY CHONKO
Holloway Professor of Marketing
Baylor University

* * *

"'Antelope or Chipmunk', what in the world could this have to do with establishing and carrying out a successful business strategy? In short, it has to do with identifying that one item that gets you excited and deep-in-the-gut passionate when you consider what it would be like to achieve it. If you have always struggled with setting goals, but more importantly achieving them, the concept of 'Antelope or Chipmunk' may be just the edge you need in mastering this sometimes difficult process."

MICHAEL R. TEAKELL, SPHR
Human Resources Manager-Wireline Division
Superior Energy Services

"Bud and Jim are dynamic personalities that have mastered the principles of motivation and sales techniques. They have achieved success at a personal and financial level in their lives, and their gems of knowledge are inspirational and easy to apply in helping us to achieve our goals and success in the business world."

SCOTT HENDON
Partner
BDO Seidman LLP

* * *

"The Profiles International assessment program has contributed significantly to the growth and development of our business here at Snap-on Tools. It has helped us to significantly improve our selection process."

TOM JOSEPHS
Director Human Resources—Dealer Group
Snap-on Incorporated

* * *

"A fantastic reference book for solving just about any business problem. Forty practical and quickly read ideas for driving a successful business."

CHARLIE MCCREEVY
Minister for Finance
Republic of Ireland

* * *

"…highlights a common sense approach to solving business challenges and opportunities. In strategy form I particularly like the piece on 'size doesn't matter if you've got the pedigree'. This should be the mantra for anybody embarking on a new venture."

DENIS O'BRIEN
CEO
Communicorp

* * *

"As Executive Director of the Texas Commission on Human Rights and subsequently as Principal of Bill Hale and Associates, I have worked with Jim and Bud for a number of years. This book has a wealth of information on successful people-oriented business strategies. These guys really know their stuff."

BILL HALE
Principal
Bill Hale and Associates

* * *

"Every page contains insightful and instructive lessons for everyone who desires to build a winning business strategy."

RONALD TREGO, PH.D.
Consultant Psychologist

* * *

"Frank, sensitive, and humorous, it is a fascinating account of winning in business...."

Ms CAREN SCHAFFER
President
Success Group LLC

* * *

"Bud and Jim have combined many of the 'Good Business' how to books into one great one...A must read for sales and management professionals."

TOM FRANKE
Vice Chairman
Raymond James Financial Corporation

* * *

"This book is a great source for practical and useful information. It is a must read for all managers—it will be on all our partners' and managers' desks."

ARNIE HONKAMP
Managing Partner
Honkamp, Krueger & Co., P.C., CPA's

* * *

"The two successful business people have finally accomplished what all readers of business strategy publications have been looking for...clearly stated, engagingly scripted, to-the-point, real-life strategies that, when applied, will offer positive results....Now it is up to each of us to determine if we want to continue chasing chipmunks, or prioritize our lives and focus on our antelopes."

CHUCK LaMOTTE
Vice President, Human Resources
White Lodging Services Corp.

* * *

"If sales & development is your core objective, *40 Strategies For Winning in Business* is a must. The way that each topic is individually presented makes it an easy read, a great reference guide for any sales library."

RICK BUTTERWORTH
Managing Director
Carlisle Group Ireland

* * *

40
Strategies

for Winning
in Business

**Jim Sirbasku and Bud Haney
with Deiric McCann**

S & H PUBLISHING COMPANY

S & H PUBLISHING COMPANY
5205 Lake Shore Drive
Waco, Texas 76710-1732
USA
Tel: (254) 751 1644
Fax: (254) 772 8155

First Edition

ISBN 0-9742221-0-0

Printed in the United States by Signature Book Printing, Gaithersburg, MD 20879

ORDERING
Quantity Sales
Discounts are available to corporations or others purchasing in large quantities. For details, please contact S & H Publishing Company at the address above.
Individual Sales
S&H publications are available through all good bookstores, from Amazon.com, and directly from S & H Publishing Company (contact details above).
College textbook/course use; orders by US trade bookstores and wholesalers
Please contact S & H Publishing Company (contact details above).

Original illustrations by Niall Murphy (niallkmurphy@eircom.net)
Copyediting, book design and layout by The Edit Room and PageWorks (emerryan@theeditroom.ie) (davidhoulden@eircom.net)
Jacket design by MIG1 Design, sean@mig1.com

Contents

Dedication

We would like to dedicate this book to all of the great people we have been associated with in our lives.

We have always believed that, as leaders and executives, we have only been average, but we have always had great individuals working with us.

What we have done is share our dreams, and others have adopted those dreams and turned them into reality.

We believe that people have always been our greatest asset—they take bad ideas and fix them. They take great ideas and expand them. People who are suited for what they do maximize their potential—others do not.

People can make or break an idea and, because people are in the habit of being who they are, it is important to select the best person who will fit the job, not the person you like best.

People make companies successful; companies do not make people successful.

Why We Wrote This Book

When we first talked about writing this book, we asked ourselves, "Does the world really need another self-improvement book?" Obviously, we decided the answer was Yes. But we wanted our book to be different, aimed specifically at developing winning strategies for business. The reason we decided to write *40 Strategies for Winning in Business* is that both of us have been life-long advocates and practitioners of personal-growth programs, classes, seminars, books, and recordings as a means of designing winning strategies for business and for life. In this process, we have seen the good, the bad and the ugly. The vast amount of material produced by hundreds of authors and speakers during the past century makes it a difficult task to find the best material. But because of our many years of experience, we knew we could save you, the reader, time and money by recommending the most important sources of the information you are seeking.

Our experience is that many authors of self-help and management books have one or two really good ideas that could be explained in a few hundred words. The rest of the book is "filler"—that is, material that expands the work to book length without adding much substance. While numerous anecdotes illustrating a main point can be entertaining, even amusing, they do not add to your understanding or enhance your depth of knowledge. With our book, we decided to capture the best ideas from a variety of sources and present them in the concise form you have in your hand.

You may be wondering who we are and why we think we are qualified to perform this task. We come from different backgrounds, but for more than 30 years we have been associated in several businesses that have resulted in both of us becoming multi-millionaires. Neither of us inherited fortunes or family businesses. What we have achieved, we have done on our own. In the process, we have operated businesses that provided and still provide employment for hundreds of people, many of whom now also enjoy substantial financial security.

Before we met, we had each achieved some levels of success. Bud had played professional baseball, graduated from college, worked for a heating and air-conditioning business in Texas, and been a salesman, and a business owner. Jim had been a high-school athlete, earned a college degree, worked as a meat-cutter in a South St. Paul, Minnesota, packing plant, a salesman, a business owner and a corporate executive.

Our paths crossed when we worked together for the same corporation. Many times during our 20-year stint, we multiplied the company's scope, sales and profits. We had an affinity for one another and our skills were complementary. We have known and associated with thousands of businesspeople and entrepreneurs. But we have seen few partnerships that work as well as the one we share.

One thing we know from experience is that opportunity knocks many times, not just once. In 1991, it knocked again for us. We started another business. One Sunday afternoon, at Bud's house, we decided to start an occupational assessment company that we named Profiles International, Inc. As of this writing, this business, started by just the two of us, has expanded to more than 60 countries worldwide. It provides employment for thousands of people, while serving tens of thousands of businesses with products that make them better so they can expand economic opportunities for more and more people.

A main ingredient in the success that we have experienced, both individually and jointly, is "advice" we received from some of the most creative and insightful business experts, and the inspirational and motivational leaders who inspire human achievement in their books, seminars and newsletters. We were in our teens when we discovered the works of authors such as Dale Carnegie, Dr. Norman Vincent Peale, and Emile Coué. Since then, we have both read hundreds of books and attended innumerable seminars, courses and classes. We are constantly searching for better ideas and better methods for doing things. The way we do business has little resemblance to what it was 10 years ago. We are involved in a constant business evolution that has impacted on our products, our corporate structure, and the manner in which we deliver our products and services to clients.

Through the years, we have had countless opportunities to associate with and learn from leaders and experts from many industries and businesses. We never miss a chance to ask questions and seek the advice of others, whether in a business or social setting. You might be surprised at what you can learn from the person in the seat next to you while flying from Dallas to New York, or while networking at a cocktail party. The point is that we have formed the habit of becoming perpetual students because we discovered that the more we know, the more we want to learn. It is a habit that has served us well.

In *40 Strategies for Winning in Business,* we have distilled the wisdom of hundreds of authors, business leaders, philosophers, Ph.D.s, speakers, teachers, preachers and personal acquaintances, along with a few ideas we came up with on our own. After considering our collective experience, we concluded that less than half of the books, seminars, classes, speakers, etc. had been worth the time. Even more significant was our conclusion that only about 20 per cent of the ideas and concepts we had learned had actual practical application in developing winning strategies. In this book, you will find the 20 per cent that, in our opinion, really mattered.

We want to thank the many people who have encouraged us to write this book. For years, our friends and business associates have asked when we were going to put what we know and have learned into a book. Finding time to do everything we want to do is always a challenge and it has taken a while for "the book" to reach the top of our priority list.

It is our sincere desire that you, the reader, will find greater success in our profession and in other aspects of your life as a result of using the ideas and techniques we have included here. We hope that *40 Strategies for Winning in Business* will inspire, motivate and lead you to loftier results. We hope that by presenting the essence of our many years of study and observation, we will make a significant contribution to your progress in designing winning strategies that work effectively for you.

Jim Sirbasku
Co-Founder
Profiles International

Bud Haney
Co-Founder
Profiles International

Strategy 1

Antelope and Chipmunks

Antelope and Chipmunks

Know Your Goals
and Focus Upon Them

Goal setting is a subject to be emphasized early in the development of a business career, and we can't emphasize it enough. We have formed the habit of setting goals daily, weekly, monthly, annually, and for the next ten years! We think you should, too.

A Personal Story from Jim Sirbasku

I learned the power of goal setting early in my career when a mentor asked me to name something I really wanted. I told him I had always dreamed of owning a Cadillac. With his coaching, I learned how to turn my dream into something I could drive. I soon learned the motivational power of visualizing my goals. I went to the Cadillac dealer's showroom and found a brochure with a picture of the exact model I wanted—a blue convertible. I cut out the picture and made copies, which I pasted in places where I would see them often every day—the bathroom mirror, the refrigerator door, the dashboard of my car, and the cover of my appointment calendar. Then, I began writing a step-by-step plan for reaching the goal. Looking at the pictures of "My Cadillac" deepened my desire and motivated me to "sell harder." When a prospect told me, "I want to think about it," I was motivated to try one, two, and three more closing questions. When I felt like quitting for the day, I would make a cold call. I prospected for people I could see on weekends or in the evening. My goal was constantly on my mind. It made me more focused on how I was using my time, and I carefully prioritized my daily tasks to make the most of every minute. I was driven by my desire to be driving "My Cadillac." In less than a year, I returned to the dealership with cash in hand, and drove away in the car of my dreams. The experience made me a confirmed goal-setter. I learned a process I have repeated thousands of times to achieve other personal and business objectives.

Here is an interesting approach to the subject of goal setting. We present these ideas so you can use them to drive the car of your dreams and obtain all of the other goals important to you, too.

Is your life an antelope hunt or a chipmunk chase?

A former world leader once used an analogy wherein he regarded himself as a lion, the head of the pride, no less, and all of the issues he ever faced as either "antelope" or "chipmunks." Even when a lion is dying of hunger, he won't give chase to any of the many smaller animals, like chipmunks, which gambol nearby, offering a quick and easy snack. Why? Even if he made the effort and caught one, and there's always an outside chance he'd fail, it simply wouldn't satisfy him. However, even when weakened by hunger to the extent that he can hardly move, when an antelope shimmers into view miles away across open plains, the sight moves the lion to action. In spite of being so weakened that he knows a failed effort could be the end of him, the lion commits to the hunt. If there's even a slight chance of success, he'll give his all because success will fill his belly for weeks to come. The greater reward is worth his all, and so he begins the long process of focused effort which he clearly envisions will end in a successful kill.

A single-minded focus upon clearly defined "antelope" is what also characterizes most successful businesspeople.

Have you identified your *antelope*? Do you hunt them every day at the expense of less-satisfying chipmunks? Look out across your plains and spot your own *antelope*.

If there's a slight chance of success, the lion commits all.

1. Think about your life or your business and write down what you'd like to achieve. Would you like to drive your company sales up to $10 million or a billion? Write a book? Hike through the Himalayas? On a single piece of paper, write down everything you'd ever like to achieve.

2. Identify the one item on your list you most want to achieve. This is your first antelope—shimmering in the heat of day, miles out on the plain of your life.

3. Focus on this first antelope. Build a clear picture of it in your mind. How will you feel when you catch it? How will it change your life? What will your loved ones say? Get a clear mental picture of exactly how the end of a successful hunt will feel. See it in full color, full detail. As

4

you sight your first antelope and begin the process of throwing your whole self into an all-or-nothing hunt, you are going to need the energy to keep you in the hunt, even when things become difficult. *That energy is passion.* Fuel your passion: review the mental picture you've built, and capture on paper all of the benefits you'll enjoy once you've run this beauty to ground. Describe every benefit in detail. The more benefits you record, the greater the passion you'll bring to the hunt.

4. If it were easy to catch antelope, we'd all dine on venison daily! At least we'd enjoy the benefits of achieving major goals daily. Life simply isn't that easy, is it? Obstacles always seem to get in the way. So now, write down every obstacle that comes to mind. What's going to stop you from bringing down your antelope? Work out precisely how you'll deal with each obstacle. Form a clear strategy to deal with every pitfall you can predict—doing so will enhance your confidence and vision.

5. Set clear deadlines in writing. Think about the various stages of a successful hunt. What must you do first? How much time will you need? What has to happen next, and when will the next stage be complete? Work your way through all of the stages of a successful hunt. Your target deadline is the date at which the last stage of your hunt is complete.

6. Now do it again. Go back to your list and find more ante-lope, and work them down to the deadline stage. Don't separate out a whole herd. Simply find one or two prime candidates. Later, as you complete one hunt, you can replace it with a new one.

7. Finally, on an index card (or using a software program of your choice), note all of your antelope as succinctly as you can (including your deadlines). Once they're written, see if you can refine them—make them even sharper and more compelling. Keep this information in sight at all times. Read it first thing in the morning and last thing at night. As you start each day, ensure that you have sched-uled some actions to take you closer to your antelope. No day should go by without moving you closer to one or all of them.

Don't allow yourself to get distracted by those easier-to-catch chipmunks—always keep your focus on those more satisfying targets way out on the plain.

Strategy 2

Are You Getting Through?

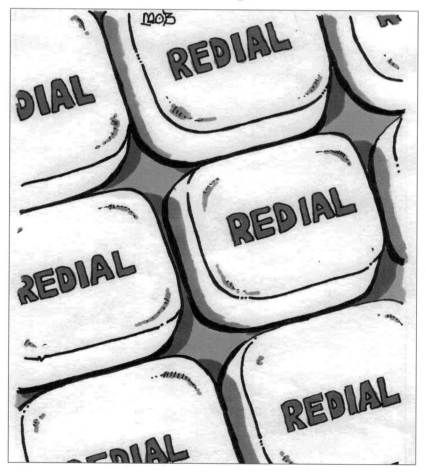

Are You Getting Through?

Making the Telephone
Work for You

The telephone is a double-edged sword: It's a tremendous tool when used properly, but it can be a source of frustration when it does not give you the results you want.

A Personal Story from Bud Haney

I recall an occasion when Jim and I conducted a training meeting focusing on isolating sales problems. One of the problems we identified was that people make dozens of telephone calls and wind up with only four or five contacts. A common occurrence was getting put into voice mail. Most of the time, it is a dead-end street. So I asked, "What do you say in a voice mail?" We found that most people leave a message like, "Hello, this is John Jones and my number is 777-4444—please call me."

One of the participants suggested a better message. "Hello, this is Pete Brown and I was talking to a friend of yours, Stan Smith, and he said I should call you. My number is 777-4444. Please call me as soon as you can."

Then, Jim and I introduced our method of dealing with voice mail. Rather than thinking of voice mail as an obstacle, we think it's a positive. Remember: "Within every adversity, there lies the seed of an equal or greater benefit." We see voice mail as a great opportunity to leave a 30-second commercial for ourselves. It's as if we had our own radio station and the undivided attention of a listener. The message can't be too long, and it must be motivational and inspirational. You have to project enthusiasm and excitement. We start the message with a provocative quote from a recognized business authority. Here's one of Jim's favorites:

> *"Peter Drucker says that 66 percent of new hires will prove to be a mistake in the first year. This is a problem, but it only gets worse because most of these mis-hired people will stay on your payroll. If you'd like a solution to this problem, give me a call. I'm Jim Sirbasku and my number is 254-751-9363."*

You want to develop voice-mail messages for all occasions so you can call back three, four or five times and leave different, but interesting, messages each time. Eventually, your unique approach is going to get results!

Now read the rest of this chapter for more ideas to help you to use the telephone effectively...because you won't always get put into voice mail!

Here's a four-step plan of action to follow when a live party answers your phone calls:

First, Greet Them

Manners are manners. Grab their attention with their name — Dale Carnegie rightly said, the sweetest sound to a person no matter what their language is their name. "*Good morning, Mr. Smith....*" Short, sweet, and to the point.

9

> *A person's name is the sweetest sound to them.*

Second, Tell Them Who You Are, Right? Wrong!

They don't care! They probably haven't heard of you or your company and, even if they have, they weren't motivated to call you. So, give them some reason to want to talk with you. Grab their attention and whet their appetites:

> *"I'm calling to tell you how we've helped Money Bank Corporation reduce staff turnover from 40 percent to just 10 percent in less than twelve months, and to see how a similar program might be of interest to you."*

The key here is research. You've got to know where they are likely to be hurting, what issues are facing this person, precisely how you can help them and, ideally, you will have a quotable example of the sort of results you've achieved for someone just like them—someone they know faces similar challenges.

Third, Only Now Do You Introduce Yourself

Now that you've got their attention and interest, they are more likely to be wondering, "Who is this?"

> *"My name is Jim Selby, and I'm calling from HR Associates."*

Fourth, Ask for an Appointment

What you have to relate to them is beyond effective discussion by telephone, so ask to meet them. Keep it succinct:

10

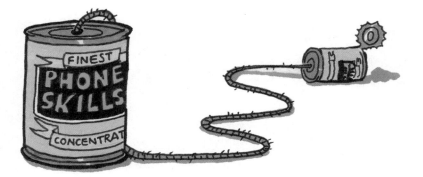

"It wouldn't be practical to take you through the benefits on the phone. Would you be available during the week of May 12th for a brief meeting?"

Always offer a specific day or week, and allow them to offer an alternative date suited to their commitments.

So, the four steps are:

1. Greeting
2. Attention Grabber
3. Introduction
4. Appointment

This simple formula is time-effective, easy to master and—most importantly—proven in practice. Use this simple proven formula to prepare every appointment call you ever make—ensuring to allow and plan for the possibility of voice mail—and you'll get to more appointments in less time than any other way.

Are we getting through?

> *"This 'telephone' has too many shortcomings to be seriously considered as a means of communication. The device is inherently of no value to us."*
>
> WESTERN UNION
> INTERNAL MEMO—1876

Strategy 3

How to Become an Employer of Choice

How to Become an Employer of Choice

Attracting and Retaining the Very Best People

While many employers complain about the difficulty of attracting and retaining quality people, other employers seem never to have this problem. What's the secret of these Employers of Choice?

In our experience, it's not really a secret. Employers of Choice simply know what's important to their prospective and current employees, and they work hard to meet those needs.

Before you can consider the challenge of attracting and retaining people, you must first look at the dark side—at what drives people from their jobs. Profiles International recently completed a survey to explore why people leave their jobs. Some employers have found the results to be fascinating. Here are the five main reasons why people change jobs:

1 Boredom

2 Inadequate salary and benefits

3 Limited opportunities for advancement

4 No recognition

5 Unhappy with management and the way they were managed.

Before we reveal the relative importance of each reason, we've got a challenge for you. Consider which of the five reasons you would address first, second, and so on, if you wanted to improve your company's reputation as an Employer of Choice. After you rank order the list, turn to the end of this strategy and see how you fared. Then continue reading here.

* * *

Were you surprised with the answers? Most employers are. The message is simple—if you want to attract and retain top people, these are the key items for consideration.

Follow these six steps and you are likely to become an *Employer of Choice*:

1. Evaluate Your Managers

The numbers don't lie. People leave people, not jobs. Look at the results—30 percent of people didn't leave their jobs; they left their managers. Poor managers can cancel out the positive effects of your heavy investment in recruitment advertising and public relations, in outstanding remuneration packages, in your excellent share option plan, and all of the other good things you do to attract and retain the right people. Your Human Resources people sweat blood to bring in a sufficient number of these right people and, in 30 percent of cases, poor managers shred them and send them back out of the company before you've even recovered the cost of hiring them. *Crazy*.

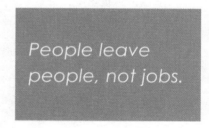

People leave people, not jobs.

So what do you do? First, start measuring your staff turnover by *manager*—pinpoint the real problems. It will frighten but enlighten you. Until you know which managers are losing their people, you can't do anything about it.

After you identify the managers who need help, help them! They can learn to become better managers. Review all of your managers in terms of their leadership and management skills. That's how you will discover what these managers are doing to drive away good people. We humbly suggest you use Profiles International's *Multi-Rater Checkpoint* to give managers, their superiors, their direct reports, and their fellow managers an opportunity to provide feedback about what they are doing well—and what they could do better. Be sure to act upon what you discover. Provide training, coaching and support to those managers who struggle to manage their people in a way that encourages productivity and retention. Good management is key to good retention.

2. Create a Recognition Culture

Insufficient recognition for the contribution they make is why 25 percent of all people leave their jobs. Fix this or learn to live with the attrition. Task your managers with the responsibility for seeking out the many ways in which their people perform above and beyond the call of duty. Have them consciously seek out opportunities for positive recognition. Create awards for exemplary performance and give everyone an opportunity to bask in the glow of positive recognition for a job well done. But be aware that a recognition culture cannot be created from nothing—it requires a healthy working environment to thrive.

3. Create a Healthy Work Environment

To encourage development of a genuine recognition culture, you'll need to create a healthy work environment. Not healthy in the sense of lots of fresh air and few toxic chemicals knocking around (although that's always a good start), but a healthy *psychological* work environment—one where providing recognition for exemplary performance seems normal. There are several key elements to achieving this.

First: **Open Communications**. There are too many old-economy attitudes abroad in our businesses. In the old economy, scarcity was the driving force—information was power, and those who had information hoarded it and kept it scarce. That way, they amassed great power, privilege and wealth. Look around—the world has changed dramatically. Our modern economy is based on abundance—those who prosper are those who share information with everyone and anyone who can make use of it effectively. This is the information age, and any environment where the workforce has not tapped into all that's going on in their organization is toxic. Suspicion, mistrust and resentment grow—and key people go.

Let all of your people know where the organization is going; how it plans to get there; how their jobs play a part in the grand scheme of things; and why they are key to your success. Their contribution is just as valuable as the CEO's, and they know it. Let them know that you know it, too. Spread information liberally throughout your organization; give your people an *I'm on the inside!* feeling—it's hard to leave something that has you on the inside.

Next, **Develop an Attitude of Cooperation**. Give and take is the order of the day. Be prepared to consider anything that makes it easier and more practical to work for you than for anyone else. Look at flexible hours, compassionate leave, sabbaticals, teleworking, childcare facilities—anything you can afford to do that shows that you are prepared to meet your people halfway (or more) in balancing their work/personal life commitments.

Finally, **Develop an Atmosphere of Trust**. If you want people to trust you (with their jobs, their careers, their development—their lives), then you have to trust them. Create an atmosphere where management automatically expects the best of its team members—they'll respond. Give people a good reputation to live up to—they won't let you down. This is one of the key sources of recognition—no one is more flattered than when they are trusted implicitly.

4. Create an Atmosphere of Continual Self-Improvement

Of the people who leave their jobs, 20 percent do so because they feel that they're not getting sufficient advancement to retain them. Not surprising, really. Flat-structured organizations don't have the dizzying promotional heights that previous generations of workers could aspire to scaling. So, there's really nothing we can do about this point unless we still have an old-fashioned multi-layer hierarchical organization, right?

No! That thinking is about as wrong as you can get.

Today's job-seekers want the opportunity to develop themselves to be all that they possibly can be—to continually polish their skills, abilities and experience so that their potential market value continually rises. And if they can do this without the uncertainty of job-hopping, then so much the better. So you don't necessarily have to have multiple promotional opportunities to meet this demand. What you need is a clear, ongoing development path—a way that each and every one of your people can advance their skills and value so that they become all that they can be. This means heavy investment in training and development.

Create an atmosphere of continual self-development— give everyone access to any training that will enhance their skills, their value, and their self-esteem. Don't be boxed in to limiting the training available to those skills specific to an individual's current job. Remember that you are not simply training for job-effectiveness but are also offering your people the development opportunities that make them feel good enough about the pace of their *personal* advancement that they don't feel the need to seek out greener grass elsewhere. Invest heavily in training and development, and then actively encourage your people to take advantage of your programs. Provide them with the means for success—train them on company time; give them study leave; let senior managers coach and support them. Engage them in their own ongoing, longer-term development. Show them how they can get all of this development from within your organization; focus their minds on genuine

> Help your people to be all that they possibly can be.

development goals that extend far beyond the availability of the next recruitment supplement. This creates truly compelling and self-serving reasons to stay.

Well done! If you implement these first four steps, you've already eliminated 75 percent of the reasons why people leave their jobs. And did you notice, we haven't even mentioned money?

5. Put Your Best Foot Forward

What about the 15 percent who leave for more money? Will more recognition, better management, and opportunities for continual self-development retain them? In many cases, yes (at least for a time). But you still have to pay the market rate or better to stay in the game. However, it's critical that you know when and how you pay this level.

As you read this strategy, chances are that you're sitting down. Good. Because the next suggestion can topple some old-style thinkers. When it comes to remuneration, put your best foot forward immediately. Pay your people as much salary, give them as many benefits as you can afford—and do it from day one.

Abandon the *"What can I get her for?"* thinking in favor of *"How much is this position worth to me, and what can I afford to pay?"* Then pay it. Let your people know that this is what you're doing, and that you need their support and effort to help you to maintain a situation where you can continue to do this in the long term—that you need them to engage with you in making the organization successful.

Think about it sensibly—if you pare back the package at offer time by the 10 or 15 percent you can get away with, will the savings be enough to retain these people in the face of an offer from another employer? Most likely not—it will be too little, too late. So, put your best foot forward—and let everyone know that you are paying absolutely as much as you can and that, to continue to do so, everyone will have to pull together as a team to generate the productivity necessary for the organization's success. We all respond to fair treatment.

Now, don't misunderstand the advice—pay as much as you can, not more than you can. Pay more than you can afford and you are likely to pay your way out of business. Our advice: Know what each job is worth, and pay it early.

6. Match People to Jobs

Having followed 360,000 people through their careers during a period of 20 years, a major study published by *Harvard Business Review* demonstrated that a key ingredient in retaining people is ensuring that they are matched to their jobs in terms of their abilities, interests, and personalities. The study found that when you put people in jobs where the demands of the job matched their own abilities, where the stimulation offered by the job matched their particular interests, and where the cultural demands of the position matched their personalities, staff turnover decreased dramatically, and productivity increased dramatically.

Use psychometric tools to determine the requirements of each of your positions in terms of abilities, interests and personality, and then use this information to match your jobs to people who will excel in them. Gut feeling cannot do this assessment for you—it needs to be undertaken using properly validated tools designed for this purpose. (*The Profile* is a business tool designed to make job matching easy, and you can learn more about it at: www.profilesinternational.com)

Once you know what each job requires, you can more effectively match people to their jobs, providing any training, support, or coaching necessary for them to be successful. Put the right person in the right job and you eliminate a large portion of the 5 percent who leave simply because they are "bored with the job."

Sadly, there is no quick, easy and inexpensive "silver bullet" to help you to win the war for quality people. But apply these six sensible steps and you can eliminate more than 95 per cent of the reasons why people defect—putting yourself well on track to be one of that envied class—the *Employer of Choice*.

How Did You Do?

The study found that of the job-leavers surveyed:

- 30% were unhappy with management and the way they managed

- 25% felt they got no recognition for good work

- 20% complained of limited opportunities for advancement

- 15% cited inadequate salary and benefits (low, isn't it?)

- 5% were bored with the job

- 5% cited other reasons (retirement, career change, sabbatical, travel).

So, if you want to attract and retain the people essential to your success, these are the key factors that you have to consider—and the priorities are abundantly clear. Money, for example, is important—but not nearly as important as most employers seem to believe.

Return to where you were in the strategy to see what you can do to make practical use of this insight.

"There is nothing more important to your success than hiring great people. Nothing."

LOU ADLER

HIRE WITH YOUR HEAD

Strategy 4

Big Dogs Expect to Win

Big Dogs Expect to Win

Fake it 'til You Make it!

A Personal Story from Jim Sirbasku

Not long ago, Bud and I were inducted into the Sales Hall of Fame, Quite and Honor! During my acceptance remarks, I used the phrase, "Fake it 'til you make it," which is a way of saying you should act like the person you want to be, until you become that person. One of the other inductees was the late Mary Kay Ash, the founder and inspirational leader of the world-famous cosmetics company. She was honored posthumously. After my remarks, her grandson approached me and asked where I had learned, "Fake it 'till you make it," because he had heard his famous grandmother say it many, many times. He told me it was something she taught all of her salespeople. She believed it had special meaning in times of adversity because no one needs to know when you are not doing well.

The rest of this chapter talks about acting the part of the Big Dog. *You may not be a* Big Dog *now, but if you're ever going to be one, it's important you think and act like one. So read on and follow the* Big Dog Code*!*

When a big dog comes on the canine scene, all of the others sit up and take notice. If there's going to be a scrap, they all know that the big dog is likely to win. But sometimes you see a fierce mini-pooch get into a dog fight and wipe out all of the competition. This happens because the mini-pooch knows the *Big Dog Code*, and follows it.

Whether you would characterize your company as a poodle or a Rottweiler, when you follow the *Big Dog Code*, you will find that you expect to win too. Here are the *bones* of the *Big Dog Code*.

Big Dogs Howl at the Moon

A full moon is the best promotional opportunity in the *Big Dog* calendar, and no pooch worth its bones misses the opportunity to let loose and let everyone know it's around. *Big Dogs* bark first, bark loudest, and keep right on barking long after all of the lesser mutts have abandoned the opportunity. Seek out as many platforms as you can to howl out the many reasons why your potential customers should sit up and take notice. There are many and, like the moon, many can come to you for free. Seek out speaking engagements at key industry events, and host or sponsor useful seminars for the industry associations involved in your marketplace. Look for opportunities to contribute articles to industry journals. When the *Big Dog* starts howling at the moon, the rest of the pack joins in eventually. All anyone remembers is the one who barks first, barks loudest, and barks consistently.

Big Dogs Don't Chase Cars

Big Dogs don't waste their time chasing cars. They leave it to the mutts. They know that even if they catch the car, they wouldn't know what to do with it. Focus your efforts on chasing only opportunities providing a worthwhile return for your efforts. Before you start chasing prospects, be sure you know what you're going to do with them when you catch them, and be sure it's worth the effort. Chase only prospects who have adequate need for your products, have the wherewithal to pay for them, and are likely to yield some kind of profit. Don't get into the habit of chasing anything that moves. Leave it to the mutts. Be cool. You can afford to be selective. You're a *Big Dog*.

Big Dogs Will Hound You Until They Get What They Want

If a *Big Dog* sees a rival with a bone he fancies, he immediately goes after it, and nothing will stop him until it's his. Even if he's greeted with a snarl and a show of teeth, he'll withdraw a little, recompose himself and come back again and again.

Research shows that most big deals close after seven customer interactions, or more; the same research shows that most salespeople give up after a single "No!" Winning the best deals takes persistence. Be a *Big Dog*. Persist until you get the deals you want.

Big Dogs Get to Know the Pack

Big Dogs get to know more of the members of their own pack and of the other packs running in their area. A great benefit of all this sniffing around is that the *Big Dog* is the first to know if someone new moves into their territory. This kind of fearless networking is key to looking like a *Big Dog*. Get out and about. Make sure you meet the maximum possible number of people in your area who might eventually be interested in what you have to offer. Find out who else is operating in your area. Get

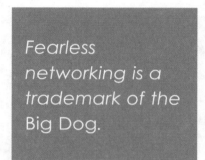

Fearless networking is a trademark of the Big Dog.

your nose right into their business and get to know what they're all about. The *Big Dog* knows everyone on his block—friend or foe. Network constantly.

There's No Mistaking a Big Dog's Territory

Big Dogs mark their territory. The *Big Dog*'s brand sends out a pungent *"Keep off! This is mine"* warning to any potential interlopers. Protect your own territory. Once you've won customers, work hard to keep them. Let them know how much you value them. Find out what it will take to retain them, and work hard to meet their needs. Then, let the world know—here are my customers; here's why they're eager to stay with me; and here's why you should be talking with me, too. Good relationship management will serve to keep other mutts out of your territory, and communication of testimonials and successful references will build your *Big Dog* reputation and help to bring in new customers. Once you win some territory, make sure everyone knows it's yours, and work hard to keep it.

Size Doesn't Matter if You've Got the Pedigree

When you're in a situation where everyone knows you're not quite as big a dog as you'd like to have them believe, remember a key rule—size doesn't matter if you've got the pedigree. Act like a thoroughbred. Be professional, adhering to a strict code of business ethics, and look after the important details. That way you'll always get the *Big Dog* respect you deserve. Professionalism and ethics are key.

Follow the *Big Dog Code*, and everyone will assume you're a big dog. Do it because you know you deserve to win!

Strategy 5

Of Course
I Remember You!

Of Course
I Remember You!

Nothing is More Important
to People than Their Names

"Hey Bud, let me introduce you to someone I've just met. This is...um...I'm sorry, what did you say your name was again?"

Embarrassing? No, that's too small a word!

Take heart! Unless you're one of a small number of people worldwide suffering from prosopagnosia—*a neurological condition rendering a person incapable of recognizing faces, in spite of having good eyesight—then the following steps will save you the embarrassment of ever forgetting anyone's name again.*

A Personal Story from Bud Haney

Almost everyone struggles with remembering the names of people they meet. I was helped when I learned that if you have empathy for people, you will have an easier time remembering their names. I think I learned this principle by observing Jim Sirbasku in action. Jim used to have a problem remembering names because his "E" was bigger than his "EM." Here's what I mean. When he met people, his focus was on himself, or his ego, which I call the "E." Jim was more focused on "telling" people than he was on "learning" from people. I decided the way to help Jim start remembering names was to remind him to, "Use your EM (empathy), not your big E." It was my way of reminding him to pay attention to people's names and what they did, and put his ego aside.

The biggest payoff for learning to remember people's names is the embarrassment you avoid.

This chapter is full of ideas to help you to improve your memory when it comes to recalling the names of the people you meet.

1. Switch Off the Internal Dialogue

As you're reading this strategy, take a moment to examine what else is flying around in your mind. It's no different in social or business situations where you're meeting people for the first time. Instead of focusing solely on the person you're meeting, your mind is filled with snatches of other concerns flying through it— *"...mmm, the food looks good...when she's finished speaking, I'm going to say...."* With all of that internal dialogue, it should come as no surprise that you find yourself embarrassed to have "forgotten" someone's name—in reality, you just didn't bother to try to

remember it in the first place. Become conscious of your internal dialogue and make a conscious effort to focus your attention exclusively on the external dialogue. Every time you find yourself drifting inwards, step out. Stay external—prepare to remember.

2. Listen

Hey, come back! Just because I'm repeating Rule #1 of good communication—a rule you've had hurled at you time after time—don't ignore this key element. Good listeners rarely forget names. Learn to listen actively by applying the next few steps which focus your active listening engine. Focus, and when a person's name is introduced into the conversation, be sure to hear it!

> *Listen!*
> *Good listeners*
> *rarely forget*
> *names.*

3. Bury the New Name in Your Memory

First, repeat it in a sentence. Plain and simple everyday courtesy phrases like, *"It's a pleasure to meet you, **Marie**"* will do it. This has two effects: firstly, it puts the name immediately into your short-term memory; secondly, it makes the new person feel good—most people love the sound of their own name. If it's an unusual name, ask her to spell it—*"...is that N-I-L-G-U-N?"* This implants it even deeper in your memory and builds further rapport. Finally, think about the name itself—does it sound like anything else? Is there any way you can make a memorable association? Names like

Wood, Holly, Marsh, Guinness or Green are made for memorable associations. If there's no obvious association, then consider what their names sounds like: McCann (My Can), Harrison (Hairy Son), Kendall (Candle). The process of trying to make these connections helps to bury names further in your memory.

4. Make Eye Contact

When meeting someone, really look at them. Make eye contact and smile. Imagine the name of your new acquaintance is written in big luminous letters across her forehead. Then observe: What makes her face interesting and different? Has she a parting in her hair, or a gap in her teeth? Eyebrows that meet? A long nose? You don't have to stare them out to do this effectively. All of this can be picked up in a few quick glances—if you're prepared to make the effort.

5. Bring it All Together

Finish the job of remembering them forever. You've got the name, you've got some memorable association, and you've got some distinguishing physical features. Now, construct a mental picture for this person. Connect their unique physical features with their name's association to create a picture that will pop into your mind next time you meet them. The sillier the picture, the better.

> Construct mental pictures to remember people's names.

35

This is an absolutely infallible system—apply it and you'll never forget someone again. With a little practice, this process becomes so automatic and instantaneous that you'll find a mental picture pops into your head instantaneously for every new person you meet—ensuring that every new face and name is filed away in your mental Rolodex. *Forever.*

Strategy 6

Where Does it Hurt?

Where Does it Hurt?

No Pain—No Gain

When you have a problem with your health, or when you simply don't feel well, you visit your doctor. Typically the doctor asks questions such as: "Where does it hurt?", "What's the pain like?" and "When did you first notice it?" The doctor doesn't necessarily expect you to know exactly what's wrong with you or how you might be cured. But your answers to questions posed by the doctor provide needed insight into the problem.

Your doctor begins by examining your symptoms, your "pains," if you will, and when you have provided as complete a picture of all of your pains as you can, the doctor has a basis to diagnose the problem. Very often, your actual pains won't directly suggest what is ultimately identified as your ailment. Equally often, the remedy prescribed won't be anything like what you might have expected.

So, how does this relate to your customers? Surely they come to you for help with their business "pains" because they view you in the same light as their doctor, an expert who specializes in helping people like them to solve their business-related problems. It's hardly reasonable to expect customers to have fully diagnosed themselves before they turn up at your office. Even if they have diagnosed themselves, surely your consultant's oath requires you to investigate their "pains" before accepting their diagnosis. You're the doctor, the expert, after all.

However, while your customers' pains may be very real, they are not necessarily accurate descriptions of their requirements.

They are merely clues to them. Clues you must collect, examine and diagnose. Once you have diagnosed the cause of these pains, you can then suggest the best course of treatment.

While you think it would be wonderful if your business never experienced any pain, it is a fact of life that every growing company has problems. That's the pain. The gain comes when you solve the problems and move on.

In this chapter we discuss business pain, how to make an accurate diagnosis, and dealing with the real problem, not just covering up the symptoms.

We once worked with a customer who was having problems keeping salespeople. The customer had tried everything. They had weekly training, they hired consultants, they increased commissions, they offered bonuses, they had contests, but sales remained flat and people kept leaving. They mistakenly believed their sales position was not attractive enough and had tried to enhance it. We assessed their entire sales staff and came to a different conclusion. We told them that our assessment showed that 60 percent to 80 percent of the people they hired were not going to succeed regardless of what they did. We did an analysis of their people who were succeeding and developed a benchmark for hiring. Now the company is hiring only people who match the benchmark, so they are hiring people who are like those with a history of success in selling their product.

In the end, developing a clear, comprehensive picture of the problem your customer is trying to solve is the most important part of your sales cycle. If you get the problem wrong, you'll get the solution wrong (and if you're still selling product, and not solutions to customer problems, then someone is going to steal away your business over time). If you can't make customers believe you understand their problem, you definitely won't convince them that your solution is superior to those offered by all other bidders—because it likely won't be.

Doctor Knows Best

So, when preparing to sell to a customer, emulate your good doctor's approach:

Question the Problem They're Trying to Solve

Working with your team, list the pains you feel your customer is experiencing. Rely on your personal experience with the customer (or competitors) and the customer's industry to make your analysis. Speculate about problems that the customer may be experiencing because of industry or economic issues. The customer may not be aware of the real issues.

Think: Commercial, Technical and Personal Pains

Commercial Pains are those associated with the general objectives for most good business decisions: to increase sales, to decrease costs, to improve market positioning. Ask yourself: *What does the customer want to achieve by solving this problem?...Why try to solve it now—what benefits will accrue?...What happens if it's not solved?...Why has the company asked me (my company) to help solve it?...Have their competitors solved this problem? How?*

Technical Pains appear when the customer tries to improve a technical process which is key to the health of their business. For example: Do they need to increase production line efficiency? Are line-machinery downtimes a real concern in their industry? Are their current systems

> *Look for Commercial Pains, Technical Pains, and Personal Pains.*

unreliable? Would faster, more modern systems improve their bottom line?

Furthermore, as all customer organizations are run by people, you must consider the impact their personal views and objectives have on the way their problems are defined. Don't forget **Personal Pains**. Anything you know of the dynamics of the politics in your evaluator group, or in your customer organization as a whole, should be noted as a "requirement." These points must also be adequately addressed by your proposal. These personal factors may not be overtly stated, and you probably won't overtly address them, but be sure to recognize them. You must take account of them.

Then, Confirm and Diagnose

Assemble the disparate list of pains into groups of related pains, and title these groups so that they make sense to the customer. For example, Price Performance, or Improved Throughput. Take this summary to your customer and confirm the accuracy of the assessment of their problem.

Having discussed your assessment with your customer, modify it as required.

Now, Cure Them

With a first-class description of your customer problem in hand, you are ready to begin to build your solution to the problem.

Follow this approach to identifying customer problems and then build all of your solutions to cure each of the pains you identify. At the very least, you can be sure that every business proposal you write will get the consideration it deserves.

Remember, Doc—no pains, no gain.

Strategy 7

First Impressions Last

First Impressions Last

Your Image is You

You've heard this before, haven't you?

You don't get a second chance to make a first impression.

This wisdom has been handed down for centuries, and yet we sometimes wonder: Is anyone paying attention? *How often have you visited a business, a professional, an advisor of some type, only to wonder how they remain in business? Some people just don't seem to care about making an impression...a good impression, that is.*

A Personal Story from Jim Sirbasku

When Bud and I started Profiles International, Inc., we rented 500 square feet of office space and sold to companies with bigger closets. We knew it was important for us to look bigger than we were, so we hired a professional firm to give us a logo that delivered an impact. We also asked them to create an image brochure to tell our story in such a way as to impress even the biggest corporations.

One day, we gathered together all of our printed material: letterhead, business cards, image brochure, etc., and Bud exclaimed, "Our image is bigger than we are!" From that point forward, we made it our mission to grow the company to be as big as our image. Of course, this has become a never-ending program of reinventing ourselves by creating an ever-growing image.

Through this evolution, Profiles International, Inc. has evolved from a pencil and paper testing company into a high-science information company. We have employed the services of skilled psychologists who develop and improve our products. Through the Internet, our products are instantly available to any of our customers all around the world.

Our company image is all about lasting impressions. Getting our image right is one of the most important exercises we undertake in assuring our success as business owners. Most people think their company's image is something largely outside of their control. It's not! Based on our experiences, as well as information we've gleaned from a variety of professionals, the following three steps will help you to build an image to foster the success you desire as a business owner.

Step 1. Identify the Image You Want to Project

Before you can build an image, you need to decide what image you want for your business. Ask yourself three questions:

What Image Should My Business Project?

If you were a banking institution, you'd most likely want to project conservatism, low risk and good standing. If, on the other hand, you were a Silicon Valley electronics company, you'd want to project an image of innovation and risk-taking. Even your family mail carrier's success depends on projecting an image of utter reliability. Decide whether you want your customers to view you as innovative, reliable, conservative, bold, progressive, traditional, professional, friendly, etc. Come up with one or two words effectively capturing the image you'd like to project.

Who are My Target Customers?

Whatever else you do, you must ensure that your image closely matches the image your target customers have of themselves. Who are your target customers? Where do they currently go for advice on products and services like yours? How much do they have to spend? Would you open a luxury hotel in a low-income area? There's simply no point in being the most expensive or best of class in your area if nobody in your area can afford to shop with you. Equally, you'd be squandering the potential (and the likely higher real-estate costs) in a high-income area by establishing a budget motel. For optimum success, be sure that there are enough of the sort of customers you'd like to target to make the business work, and that the image you decide to project matches your target customers closely enough to attract them to you.

> *Your image should spring from what your target customers expect.*

Who is My Competition?

Look at the image of your most successful competitors. If you have an outstandingly successful competitor, figure out which aspect(s) of their image fosters their success. Are they very reliable? Have they a strong service orientation?

46

Have they an incredibly wide range of products? You'll want to adopt positive elements of their image, and enhance them with whatever you feel makes your business special. If your competitor offers an extraordinarily wide range of products and you do too, you can adopt that aspect of their image, but enhance it with another feature of your business. For example, in addition to the wide product range, let's say you also create a reputation for extremely friendly service. Don't try to compete with a successful competitor's image head on. Always find some additional aspect to make your image special, if not unique.

Step 2. Build an Identity that Projects Your Desired Image

Once you know what sort of image you'd like to project, it's time to build a vehicle, an identity, which will allow you to project your new image effectively.

Start with a Logo

A good identity is about consistency. All of the ways in which you communicate with your customers must have a consistent and considered look and feel. Look and feel begins with a good logo. There are many other aspects to a company identity, but few are more important than the logo. When it appears over your door, on your business card, on your letterhead, in advertisements, and on brochures, your logo should instantly convey your desired image. For this reason, designing a logo is not for the lay person. Get professional help. There is a myth that designers are very expensive to work with—this needn't be so. Besides large graphic-design studios that might cost a little more, there are many freelance graphic designers who will work with you to help you to craft a logo that works well for you. You'll find plenty of designers in the Yellow Pages. Don't skimp on your logo. In the long run, poor communication of your image will cost you more than a designer ever will.

> *Don't skimp on getting your image right— it's false economy.*

Working with Designers

Designers are like lawyers and other professionals. They work better when you have a plan for them to follow. Before you sit down with your designer, brainstorm about the basics of your required logo. Doing so will save your designer time, and thereby save you money.

The main elements you need to think about are:

- Taglines

  Slogans often accompany a logo. We all remember *"Pepsi Cola Hits the Spot,"* and Avis *"tries harder."* These one-liners are intended to enhance the message portrayed by the logo, and to make it more memorable. Developing a one-line catch phrase BEFORE meeting with a designer can make the designer's job easier.

  Think of the main aspect of the image you feel sets your business apart from your competitors, and will appeal most to your customers. If you emphasize the family in your business, then your tagline might be something like: "Not just a garden center—a family center." Build a six- or seven-word catch phrase around whatever is the key aspect of the image you want to foster. If you have a tagline in place, the designer will know how to create an image projecting your message.

- Color

  Color is an important part of the image your logo communicates. Reds, yellows, oranges and other bright colors tend to suggest pioneering, trendsetting and fun; while blue, grey and darker greens tend to suggest a quieter, conservative image. Look at the dominant colors in bank logos—they say it all. What colors are appropriate to the image you've selected? Be careful not to be swayed by colors you like personally but are at odds with your image. A good way to begin is by thinking carefully about the sort of colors you certainly *don't* want to use. This will be of great help to your designer.

- Typefaces

  The image conveyed by the more formal typefaces used in newspapers is vastly different from that projected by simple cursive typefaces, which is, in turn, different from the image portrayed by heavily stylized modern

alphabets. The typeface you choose is one of the strongest image cues your logo can provide. If you know what sort of image you want to project, your designer will be able to advise you about appropriate typefaces.

- ● Graphics

  Designers are very adept at producing clever graphical representations of the message you want to convey. If you decide to use a graphic element in your logo, be sure that it is easy to understand, and that the logo still communicates your message even if a potential customer doesn't "get" the point of your graphic. In other words, use graphics to enhance the words used to convey your image. Don't let the graphic dominate. It could confuse and project the wrong image.

Step 3. Once You Have Your Identity— Use it to Project Your Image

It's time to start using your new identity to build your image.

Use Your Logo Everywhere

Your logo is at the heart of your company's identity, and it will successfully communicate your desired image only if you use it effectively. Your logo must appear on all signage, vehicles, letterheads, invoices, business cards, envelopes, packaging, staff uniforms, anything issued by your company. Look for all opportunities to use your logo in everyday situations. For example, there are many inexpensive, easy-to-use graphics programs that allow you to produce first-class marketing materials with little effort. Use them!

Be Sure that Your Employees Buy Into the Image

A key to projecting a consistent image to your customers is ensuring that your employees understand the image you are trying to project, what values it encompasses, and how it translates into everything they do. This needs to be integrated into every aspect of your business, from the way you answer the telephone to the way you deal with customers on a day-to-day basis.

"Can I Change My Existing Image?"

Absolutely. If you have an established identity that has failed to build the image you desire to the level you'd like, change it. You may be concerned that some elements of your existing identity are successful in their own right, and still relevant. For example, your logo may already be quite well known, even if it's not quite conveying precisely the image you'd like. Work out which parts of your current identity you'd like to retain, and then go through the exercise of creating your identity in the manner discussed above. When it comes to logo redesign, you'll find that working with your designer to come up with a new logo to fit your new idea of the identity you require, but still retaining the better elements of your previous identity, is a lot easier than you might have expected.

> *It's key that your team understands the image you need to project.*

51

Your company image is something you need to review regularly as your business grows and expands, and your target customers mature or change. Take a look at your image on a regular basis. Is the image you're projecting still what you need? Is the identity that got you to where you are now appropriate to your development over the next few years? If not, fine-tune it.

Your business' image is one of your most important assets. The small investment of time, effort and money you make in it now will realize far greater returns long into the future. Invest in your image and make a lasting impression, a good impression the first time, every time.

Strategy 8

Fire 'em Up!

Fire 'em Up!

21 Days to a Winning, Motivated Team

Will you give ten minutes each day for the next 21 days to fire up your team like never before?

The sooner you can get a new employee into productivity, the better off you will be. At Profiles, our managers have learned the following techniques for managing and motivating people, which take the usual new-employee orientation to a higher level. This program has been successful in integrating our new team members into the Profiles culture in just 21 days, or about one calendar month. Not only has using this system accelerated the productivity of new team members, but it has proved excellent in making them feel wanted, appreciated, and accepted. Based upon the excellent results we have experienced, we heartily recommend you to implement a similar program in your company.

Here's a distillation of all you need to know to motivate people—it's drawn from all of the great writers on the subject—along with a simple 21-day plan.

Employees Want Management They Can Look Up to—Not Management that Looks Down on Them

An honest respect for all, a genuine recognition that everyone has something good to offer—this is at the heart of the successful motivator. Without respect, so-called motivation becomes manipulation—and manipulation is never successful in the long term. If you or your managers cannot show respect for your people, then, before you invest time and energy in motivational efforts, get someone who can—and have them read on from here!

Take an Interest in the Career and Personal Goals, Aspirations, Interests, Lives and Families of Those Who Work with You

No one cares how much you know until they know how much you care—about them! "Motivation" is about giving your people a "*Motive* for ac*tion*." Understand what your people value and you can more easily formulate a way in which doing what you need them to do will help fulfill not just your goals, but theirs. Take an honest interest in every one of your people and the means to motivate them will become readily apparent. Make it a goal to learn something new about at least one of your people—every day.

The Best Way to Knock a Chip off a Person's Shoulder is to Let Them Take a Bow

Do you know anyone who complains about getting too much recognition or praise for a job well done? *Do you?* Yet, research consistently shows that people will go to extraordinary lengths for a leader who takes the time to catch them doing something right and, when they do, provides them with sincere praise

> The best way to knock a chip from a person's shoulder is to let them take a bow.

55

and recognition in front of their colleagues. Praise and recognition are more motivating than money or any other single thing we can give to the people we lead.

Don't Criticize, Condemn or Complain

Dale Carnegie nailed it with this gem. When you must draw attention to poor performance, don't criticize—coach. Don't pick upon what is being done wrong, but focus all of your attention on the new behavior or action that will put things right; and always finish with a positive comment to let them see that the reason you've raised the matter is that you have seen they are capable of so much more. Correct the errant action, provide some positive feedback, and then forget it. Act like you expect better performance next time—and you'll get it.

Request—Don't Order

Real leaders lead from the front—they don't need to push from the back. Everyone rebels to some extent against being "bossed around." No one minds being asked to help.

Discuss—Don't Argue

Maturity is being able to disagree agreeably.

Be Careful with Humor

Avoid any kind of demeaning humor. If there's the slightest chance of being misunderstood, keep it to yourself. "If in doubt, leave it out."

Listening is the Greatest Compliment You Can Pay Anyone

Our opinions are all sacred to us. Listen—and hear the concerns of your people.

Most Importantly of All...

Model the behaviors, attitudes and morale level you expect others to display—show them it works.

21-Day Action Plan

Why 21 days? Research shows that it takes 21 days to establish a habit. Take the topics discussed above and apply them for 21 days. You will discover that by the end of this period, you will be doing  all of these things naturally. And the level of motivation in your team in general—even in your "toughest cases"—will be at an all-time high.

To implement your plan:

1. *Create a table* with each employee's name down the left-hand side, and each of the motivators listed above across the top. Rule your table so each person has a box against each motivator.

2. *Target improvements.* Copy this strategy and put it in a place where you can review it daily. Each day, make a determination to apply each motivator as often as possible with as many members of your team as you can. Plan to speak to each of your team members often enough to get to know what turns them on and off; determine to catch them doing something right; praise them in front of their colleagues; listen to their opinions, and so on. At the end of each day, put a tick mark in your table for each motivator you effectively applied with each team member.

Make sure your table is filling evenly with marks—make sure all motivators are being applied across the whole team. Be careful not to fall into the trap of simply working with those you already get along with, those you like, those who are in least need of some real motivational lift, or with the motivators that come most naturally to you.

3. *Review and Repeat.* At the end of your first 21-day period, stand back and admire the difference you'll have made. Pat yourself on the back, and start all over again. Select the next person you need to target specifically, and start a new table for the team at large.

Motivation is easy—if you care enough to put in a little extra effort. Anyone can motivate, and anyone can be motivated. All it takes is the right person in the right place, managed by someone who cares. Invest a little of your time over the next 21 days and fire 'em up like never before.

Strategy 9

Talk 'em Down!

Talk 'em Down!

Make Customer Complaints
Work for You

One day, we received a call from one of our Strategic Business Partners who said she was about to lose her biggest client because of a glitch in our e-mail system. How did this happen?

The first step in fixing the problems was to gather facts. The e-mail problem had originated when we installed new software not properly configured. The situation got worse when the client called our office seeking technical assistance and was given instructions that didn't work.

We quickly called a meeting of the people involved and soon had a temporary solution to use until we developed a permanent solution. Our Operations Vice President implemented the appropriate actions immediately. We called the Strategic Business Partner and gave her an update on the situation. Next, we contacted the client and explained our situation, apologized for the inconvenience, and presented the temporary solution. We not only saved the account, we were also complimented for how quickly we responded to the situation. Through quick attention to the problem and attention to the client, we turned a potentially bad situation into a very positive one.

We recommend you to consider customer complaints in a positive frame of mind and see them as suggestions for improving your products and the way you do business.

No matter how good you and your people are, or how good your products/services are, you will occasionally encounter an angry customer. A normally reasonable, happy customer who gets angry transforms into a flesh-eating beast, bent on your destruction. Sometimes they come at you foaming at the mouth and demanding satisfaction. How do you talk 'em down from the ceiling?

There are two traditional ways. The first is to eat crow immediately, accept the blame fully, beg forgiveness, kiss up, and do everything the customer-turned-beast asks in order to satisfy them. You'll likely keep the customer, but after you've crawled like that more than a few times, can you look at yourself in the mirror and smile?

Another approach is to get angry back at the customer, slug it out with them (verbally, at least), exchange blame and insults, deny all responsibility and tell them where to get off. That way you needn't worry about repeat complaints. After all, no customers, no complaints.

Calming angry customers and resolving complaints to their complete satisfaction need not mean sacrificing your self-respect. Experts have demonstrated that the following guidelines will resolve more problems more easily, and turn a complaint into a more positive experience for the customer. And you will still be able to look at yourself in the mirror and smile!

1. It's Your Problem, But Don't Take it Personally

It may not be your fault, but it's still your problem. Approach all angry customers with this attitude. Even if it is your fault, don't take the complaint personally. Customers complain because they want you to address a perceived shortcoming—not because they don't like you. Resist the temptation to fight back. Even if you win the battle, you'll lose the war. And the customer.

> *It may not be your fault— but it's still your problem.*

2. Listen

In order to address the customer's problem, you'll need to know exactly what the problem is. As with all other endeavors, listening is a key skill. Shut up and listen carefully. Besides giving you some insight into the reason for the customer's distress, it also helps to exorcise some of the initial anger the customer is feeling.

3. Don't Interrupt

Let complainants express themselves. Don't stop them midflow. Let them vent their anger; it will be easier to reason with them afterwards.

4. Calm Your Complainant and Clarify the Problem

When your customer has finished complaining, show some empathy. Explain that you understand why they're so upset, and you're going to try to sort things out. Then clarify your understanding of their problem. Ask questions and qualify comments. This will calm them and ensure that your suggested solution will address all aspects of the perceived problem. Step into your customer's shoes. Look at your company, your products, their problem and your actions from their perspective, and then decide whether or not their complaint is justified.

5. If it's Your Fault, Say So. If it's Not, Don't

When you fully understand the complaint, decide whether or not your company is at fault. Don't automatically accept blame before you know it's warranted. But if it is clearly your fault, admit it early in the process. Accept responsibility and don't hide; don't try to pass the buck. Adopt a genuinely humble tone.

6. Solve the Problem

Think about how best to solve the customer's problem. If you need some time to come up with a response, tell them so and commit to getting back to them on a specified timetable, and do so. Make sure all of your responses project a clearly concerned but calm manner. Stress your eagerness to resolve the problem, and project a calm confidence that you are the person to do it. When you have a suggested solution, agree with the customer the steps you'll take and the timeframe for correction. Assure the customer that you'll take personal responsibility for seeing the resolution through, and do so. Nothing is more important than resolving customer complaints. Attend to them with the utmost urgency. Research shows that it costs as much as ten times more to recruit a new customer than to retain one you already recruited.

7. Don't Accept Abuse

Don't accept it if a complainant steps over the line between the reasonable right to complain and outright personal abuse. Calmly explain that you will address problems, but you can do so only if they speak and act courteously and respectfully. If they continue with their abuse, terminate the conversation. You don't need that kind of customer!

8. Pin Down Moving Targets

If you're dealing with a problem that seems to grow every time you implement an agreed solution, ask your customer to put the complaint in writing so you can better understand and address it. This will help you to focus upon an agreed solution. Also, working things out on paper can sometimes make a complainant recognize if theirs is an unreasonable viewpoint.

9. Stop It from Happening Again

Try to prevent angering customers in the future:

- At purchase time, let your customers know it is your policy to resolve any difficulties they might encounter with their purchase. Then, should they call to complain, their stress levels should be a little lower given their confidence of receiving good support.

- Keep in touch. If something's about to happen that might upset customers, let them know before it's an issue.

- When a customer identifies a problem, change what you do to minimize the chance of the problem recurring.

Customers who take the time to complain are generally telling you they want to continue doing business with you, but with some changes. Put a high priority on resolving their difficulties, but don't ever feel you must sacrifice your own self-esteem to do so.

"The art of life is to show your hand... You may lose by it now and then, but it will be a loss well gained if you do. Nothing is so boring as having to keep up a deception."

E.V. LUCAS

Strategy 10

Customers for Life

Customers for Life

How Much are Your Customers Really Worth to You?

One of the most important lessons we've learned in business is that existing customers are the most valuable asset of any business. This fact is lost on most business owners and managers. Their brand, their reputation, their people, their products or services, and their cash flow are always mentioned but never a mention of their customers! This is a huge mistake, but a common one, because few business owners and managers understand the real value of their customers.

Knowing the *lifetime value* of customers is key to helping you to make important decisions about how much you can afford to spend to recruit new customers, and, perhaps more importantly, how best to go about increasing the earnings you achieve from each customer.

What is Lifetime Value?

The lifetime value of a customer is the amount they will contribute to your bottom line over the span of your business relationship with them. Before you can calculate the lifetime value of a typical or average customer, you need to consider the following:

What's the Value of an Average Sale?

For this exercise, simply divide your total sales revenue by the total number of sales for a given time period—i.e. a quarter, a half-year or a year. Let's say the average sale is $100.

What's Your Percentage Profit Margin?

Let's assume a 20 percent profit margin. It's important, however, for you to calculate the real number for your business. What's the percentage of gross sales you bring to your bottom line?

How Often Do Customers Buy from You?

Divide the total number of sales by the total number of customers for a given time period—i.e. a quarter, a half-year, or a year. Let's use three times per year for our exercise.

What's Your Typical Customer's Lifespan?

How long will a customer continue to do business with you? If you're not sure, contact your trade association. Often, trade associations conduct studies on customer longevity. Typically, in the United States, the lifespan of a customer is about seven years. However, the number can vary greatly depending on the geographic location of your business, and the demographics of your customer base. For our example, we'll use seven.

How Many Referrals Will a Customer Give You in a Year?

Referrals are leads existing customers send your way. When customers are happy, they tend to refer more often. Of course, you want as many referrals as possible because they dramatically reduce your customer acquisition costs. It's reasonable to expect at least five referrals annually from existing customers, so we'll use five in our exercise.

How Good Are You at Closing Referred Sales?

How many of these referrals become your customers? Your percentage should be very high, because a referral has been pre-sold on your business. But to be conservative, and to take into account that not all business owners sell equally, we'll use 50 percent.

Calculating the Lifetime Value

Armed with the above information, you can now calculate your typical customer's lifetime value.

Here's a chart, borrowed from our friend, Dr. John P. Hayes (www.hayesworldwide.com). It will help you to quickly calculate the lifetime value of your customers. We've put in the numbers above to demonstrate this exercise.

A. Average Value of a Sale Per Customer	$100
B. Number of Sales Per Customer Annually	3
C. Number of Years Customer Buys from You	7
D. Gross Annual Sales Per Customer (AxB)	$300
E. Gross Lifetime Revenue Per Customer (CxD)	$2,100
F. Number of Customer Referrals Annually	5
G. % of Referrals Who Become Customers	50%
H. Total Number of Referral Customers (FxG)	2.5
I. Gross Sales From Referrals (ExH)	$5,250
J. Gross Lifetime Revenue (E+I)	$7,350
K. Net Lifetime Value (JxProfit Percentage, .20)	$1,470

On average, in our exercise, a customer contributes gross lifetime revenue of $2,100. In addition, the customer generates the equivalent of another two-and-a-half customers for your business, resulting in $5,250 more gross revenue. Add the original customer's contribution to the revenue generated by the referred customers (in our exercise, $2,100 + $5,250) and the average customer is responsible for generating gross lifetime revenue of $7,350. We used a 20 percent profit margin; thus, $1,470 falls to the bottom line in this example.

That's an eye-opening number for many business owners. The good news is it's not the entire story. We calculated the referrals for only one year! A satisfied customer is likely to generate another two-and-a-half customers a year for six more years. Wow! That's another 15 customers!

A customer's lifetime value becomes even more impressive if you factor in inflation as well as the reduction of customer acquisition costs because of the number of referred customers buying from your business.

Lifetime value demonstrates how important it is to make conscious efforts to retain and develop existing customers. In our example, you would need 21 customers to generate sales of $2,100 a year if you only made one sale per customer. When you consider what it costs to recruit a new customer, and compare it to what it costs to get the same customer to buy from you repetitively, you can easily see that it's difficult to make money without repetitive sales. You need to keep your customers coming back!

Once you know a customer's lifetime value, it's easy to calculate how much money you can afford to spend to recruit a new customer. How much are you willing to spend for a customer who generates a lifetime net revenue of $1,470 for your business? Would you spend $50? Of course! How about $150? Yes. Would you spend $500? Probably, but it's not likely you'd have to. However, most business owners and managers really don't know how much they are paying for a new customer, let alone how much they should pay.

The lifetime value figure also points up just how you could dramatically improve the performance of your organization simply by making small efforts to change any of the key figures used to derive it.

Suppose you made the following modest changes to your business:

- Increase the Average Sale value by 10 per cent.

- Improve the Profit Margin by just 5 per cent.

- Increase the number of sales per year.

- Stretch the lifespan of a customer.

- Increase the number of referrals by 20 to 40 per cent.

These modest changes would result in dramatic increases for any business. Do the calculations and see for yourself how your business would benefit!

Lifetime Value is a useful customer barometer. Use it! Most of all, be sure that you and everyone in your organization understand the value of your existing customers.

Strategy 11

Dare to be Different

Dare to be Different

Differentiation is Key

Are you a "Me too?"

Do your prospective customers know why they should buy from you rather than from your competitors?

If your customers can't see any significant difference between you and your competition, the only reliable basis you'll have for winning business consistently is price—and that road ultimately leads to disaster. Selling on price is selling to your competitors' strengths.

As a company, Profiles has never attempted to compete based on price. Our intention is to offer our customers the highest-quality products we can produce at a fair price. We focus on value because people know quality and value when they see it. If a low price is a company's primary competitive advantage, we think that business is only as smart as its dumbest competitor.

We have further differentiated Profiles by our interesting and independent customer service philosophy. We believe that the best service in the world is no service at all. In other words, if your product always works well and is of the finest quality, no further service is required. Everything we do, everything we build, and everything we work on is done with the intention that only a bare minimum of customer service will ever be required.

We also believe that business goes where it is wanted and stays where it is appreciated. For this reason, a large part of our customer service has to do with showing our customers how much we appreciate them and that they do business with us. We also seek to gain their loyalty by continually demonstrating the excellent return on investment they receive because they use our products. The motto of our customer service department is, T E A M: Together Everyone Achieves More.

We know that all of our customers assign a value to Profiles and our products. We are well aware of the value we intend to deliver to them, but all customers are not created equal. We also assign a value to our customers. Although we strive to provide a high level of service to all of our customers, we are aware that we have to generate a certain level of income from each customer to justify our expenditure on service. We view the service we provide to customers as an investment in the future of Profiles.

You can differentiate your offerings using the following four steps.

1. Look at How You Stack Up to Your Competition

What can you do that they can't? What do you do distinctly better? What can they do that you can't? Look at your product or service under five main headings, seeking your particular strengths and your competitors' particular weaknesses.

Price

Are your products more or less expensive? Are you considered to be at the top, middle or low end of the spectrum in your market? Is your pricing policy something that sets you apart from your competitors?

Customer Service

Is your customer service unique? Do you provide more implementation assistance? Better ongoing back-up? Friendlier staff? More attractive terms of service? Better delivery? And so on.

Customers

Who are your best customers? Who are the people for whom you can do the best job and still make a respectable margin? Are you best with large, medium or small customers? Do you fare better in long-term relationships or short-term flings? Are you local, national or international (or all three)? Who are your ideal customers?

Product/Service

Are your products or services superior to those of your competitors? Are they faster, more efficient, quieter, easier to understand or use, or quicker to set up? Anything that's unique about your product or service is an advantage.

Reputation

What's your brand reputation like? How well known is your brand? By whom? For what? Who is traditionally attracted to your offerings?

This exercise should ideally involve anyone in your organization who will have an insight into how you stack up against your competition. Resist the temptation to do it alone—the more minds, the merrier. As you work through the exercise, capture your outcome on paper. For each of the five categories above, capture your analysis on a sheet with two columns—Strengths and Weaknesses.

The mistake most people make at this stage is differentiating their business according to the category in which they are most strongly positioned against their competitors. This is a mistake for it fails to take account of the most important person of all—your customer.

2. Become Your Customer and Think "WIIFM?"

If you fail to consider your customer's perspective, you are doomed to failure from the start. Put yourself in your customer's shoes, and ask yourself, "What is most important and valuable to me when I look for products and services? In other words, as the customer you are asking, "What's In It For Me (WIIFM)?" Be sure you have a good feeling for what your customers are REALLY looking for. Find out what they VALUE—in order of importance.

> Do customers or prospects know why they should buy from you rather than from a competitor?

Don't assume that you know what your customers want—ask them, and then LISTEN. If they say they need a good accountant, ask them what that means. What makes the difference between a good accountant and a mediocre one? If they say they want good back-up service, be sure that you understand what they mean by that.

3. Now Decide How to Differentiate Yourself

Analyze the five factors that you considered above. Which category is by far the strongest—the one with the most compelling list of strengths and fewest weaknesses? Which category ranks second, third, and so on? Now, from your research with your customers, which of these categories offer the best VALUE to your customer—which will they be most interested in? There's no point in presenting yourself as the lowest price if your customer thinks that price is immaterial—it's quality and service that count; or there's no point in stressing your excellent back-up service if the customer can't afford your price.

You'll know you've been successful when you've identified some categories of strengths that represent areas in which you are truly strong; with attributes that your customer truly values; and unique attributes that your competition cannot easily copy. Always try to identify more than one category, and rank them in value as differentiators. Remember—not everyone will be impressed by the same message.

4. Focus Your Marketing through the Lens of Your Differentiators

You know what sort of messages you need to communicate about your products or services to ensure that you grab the attention of your target market; you know what messages will most effectively differentiate your business from your competition. Now ensure that these are the only messages communicated by your public relations, advertising, sales collateral, your sales force and your support force. Don't confuse your target customers by sending conflicting messages. Continually position yourself as the number one, the expert in your particular sphere of differentiation.

However, be sure to repeat Step 2 on a reasonably regular basis. Customer values evolve, and so must your basis for differentiation. Differentiation is an ongoing process.

Follow these suggestions and your prospects will know what you do; how what you do is better than what your competitors do; why they should buy from you first; and what's in it for them if they do. This is your competitive advantage. Dare to be different and you can really start to win in business.

> *"In order to be irreplaceable, one must always be different."*
>
> CoCo Chanel
> (1883–1971)

Strategy 12

Sizzling Hot Mail

Sizzling Hot Mail

Get Your Prospect's Attention

Most sales letters and mailers never get opened...they are dropped directly into the trash. How do you prevent your sales messages from sharing this fate? Take some direction from AIDA. You probably recognize AIDA as the title of a popular opera, but AIDA is also the secret to writing sales messages that get results.

A*IDA* tells you to:

- Grab their Attention and

- Provoke their Interest

- So that they'll Desire

- Taking the Action you want from them.

Grab Their Attention

Most unsolicited mail is opened over the trashcan for faster processing—and unless you have a strategy to break your reader's distraction at this point, all of the wonderful sales copy you sweated over may as well be mailed in your own trashcan—saving you the cost of a stamp.

Grabbing attention begins with the envelope. In fact, the decision as to whether or not you will open or trash a piece of mail is made within a matter of seconds. When you receive an envelope, how do you look at it? First, you look at how it's addressed. Is your name spelled correctly? Are your name and address handwritten? Is there a label below the name and address? If you answer No, No and Yes, that piece of mail goes immediately to the trash!

If the piece of mail survived so far, you next glance to the upper left corner of the envelope to see who's sending it. If you don't recognize the name, or if there is no name, you might open the envelope. If you recognize the name as some-one you don't want to hear from, or someone who has previously sent you junk mail, the letter goes to the trash.

Hand-addressed envelopes get opened more often than professionally typed envelopes. A hand-addressed envelope without a return address gets opened even more often (because the recipient is curious)! Our associate, Dr. John Hayes (www.HayesWorldwide.com), who teaches marketing principles to small business owners, says customers often say to him, "But it's not profes-sional to send an envelope without a return address. And hand-addressed doesn't look as good as typewritten." John's answer: "Do you want to look professional, or do you want to get your mail opened?" You may have written the greatest sales message ever, but if the people who receive your mail don't even bother to open the envelope, what's the point?

Attention
Interest
Desire
Action

Once the envelope is opened there's still no guarantee the letter won't get trashed. If it looks like a typical sales letter,

it will get trashed. But if it grabs attention, it's likely to get read.

Direct mail experts say the best way to get attention is with a large, bold headline at the top of the page. This is the single most important feature of your letter. But what do you put in a headline? Try one of these ideas:

- **Ask a Question**—one that your reader instinctively wants to answer "Yes!" to.

- **Make a Promise**—"*Reduce your business phone bill by 75% immediately.*"

- **Give Them News**—"*Using AIDA increases sales-letter hit rates by 1,000%!*"

- **Tell Them "How to"**—"*How to have that perfect figure for the beach this summer.*"

- **Provide a Testimonial**—"*Last year, I couldn't even spell tecknishun and now I am one thanks to Online Learning.*"

Brainstorm with your colleagues and friends to come up with as many possible headlines as you can. Then narrow down the list to the best one by running it past as many people as you can—look for the headline that they think would grab their attention (but don't throw away the rejects—you'll see that you may need them later). When you've got your headline, you're one step closer to more sales: you've got something that will make your prospect read your letter—and that's a pretty good start.

Now Get Them Interested

After grabbing their attention, you have to describe exactly what it is you can do for your reader. How does your offering work? What does it do? How is it different from others that they might have heard about? Why should they be interested? Outline precisely what benefits the particular features of your product will deliver to them. How could your program get them in perfect shape in time for summer? How will you "reduce their business phone bill by 75%?" Tell them what you can do for them—and then prove it using compelling examples, testimonials from satisfied customers and successful case histories.

Create a Desire

Now you need to to make them desire what you're offering. This means putting the benefits of your offer in terms that mean something to them personally, that will make them desire your offer enough to take the next step with you. Show them how they will feel on the beach if they do have "the perfect figure this summer." What will they be able to do with the money saved on phone bills? What will it be like to write sales letters that get a ten times better response? How will their new career as a technician change their lifestyle? Use specific datelines and details to make your point: *"...if you start now, by June 1st you could be back in a size eight"..."...join our course by January and you could be earning $45,000 as a technician by year end"..."...start now and you could double your sales for Q3."* Make them want you, and then...

Ask Them to Take Action

What do you want them to do when they finish reading your letter? "Many times, letters fail to explain how to take action," explains Dr. Hayes. "Or they don't give the reader enough options for taking action. For example, you might tell people to call you...but what if they want to send a fax, or reply by mail, or go to a website? Be sure to give people a variety of options for contacting you and buying from you." Don't expect prospects to figure it out for themselves—be clear and specific. Tell them how they can act upon the desire you've created. Create a sense of urgency, of *"act now!"* Make it as easy as possible.

Many people think that if you can't say it in a page, you shouldn't send a letter. But they're wrong. People read long letters, especially if the letter describes something they want to buy! The more information, the better! Take as much space as you need to describe your offer, attractively. Be sure to include the benefits of your offer—what's

Take as much space as you need to describe your offer, attractively.

in it for the customer? Do not ramble, however. When you've said it all, shut up!

Don't expect to get it right the first time, every time. Before you commit to mass mailings, run test batches with a few variations on headlines and content—and fine-tune until you find the one that pulls the maximum response.

P.S.

Always have one—a P.S., that is. People see and take notice of headlines and postscripts. Your P.S. is a great opportunity to reiterate why they need to act now—restate your key selling points or benefits or, if you offer a "no-risk guarantee," state it here. Give the P.S. as much time and consideration as your headline. A good P.S. is vital in building real sizzlers.

Think *AIDA* and sizzling sales letters are just a little hard work away.

"In the modern world of business, it is useless to be a creative original thinker unless you can also sell what you create. Management cannot be expected to recognize a good idea unless it is presented to them by a good salesman."

DAVID M. OGILVY

Strategy 13

Watch Your Mouth!

Watch Your Mouth!

Be on Your Prospects' Lips

A trusted friend tells you to go and see the latest Tom Cruise movie, that it's your type of story—great acting, a wonderful script, and so on. Chances are that next time you're planning on seeing a movie, you'll take your friend's recommendation—right? We all like the comfort of a recommendation or a testimonial when we're about to invest time, effort, or money—however small the amount. Word-of-mouth can make or break movies—and just about any other business.

One of the best things you can do to promote your business is to use word-of-mouth marketing. Here's how:

Whose Mouths Can You Enlist?

Friends and Family

There's an unwritten rule that says we shouldn't "mix business with pleasure," but what if what you have to offer is better than they could possibly get elsewhere? You could be doing your friends and family a favor by giving them the opportunity to do business with you. Once you do a good job for them, they'll want to talk about it.

Existing Customers

If someone continues to do business with you over a long period, it's probably because you're doing something good for him or her. Remind yourself and them of the value of your relationship. Encourage them to say good things about you to their contacts—and to tell you when they do!

Prospects

There can be a wide variety of reasons why a prospect is not currently a customer—timing, budget, long-term commitments to other suppliers, etc. If your prospects like what you have to offer, seek referrals from them—everyone likes to give their friends help in identifying good suppliers

Suppliers

Adopt the attitude that you "do business with people who do business with you." OK, so not all of your suppliers will be able or inclined to jump right into a relationship with you,

> Everyone likes the comfort of a recommendation when they're about to invest some time, effort or money—however small the amount.

but they should surely be able to help you with some referrals to other customers of theirs who might be able to use your services. Your bank manager and accountant are good starting points.

Networking Organizations

Business Network International and Business Link are designed specifically to foster the development of referral networks. In the case of BNI, only one representative from each profession or class of supplier can join a given chapter. They meet weekly to advise their fellow chapter members about how best to sell them into their personal networks. Your local Chamber of Commerce also likely sponsors networking events that give you an opportunity to improve your word-of-mouth image. If you don't belong to a networking group, then join one now—otherwise, rest assured that a competitor is getting the jump on you.

Get Involved Yourself

Tell People about the Value of Referrals to You, and Them!

Give examples of referrals where the source of the referral also benefited from the introduction—perhaps by a cash payment, or a free product or gift. Explain that it's only by referrals that your business can prosper.

Use Testimonials

Seek testimonials from satisfied customers—ask them to write you a letter and explain how their relationship with you has been of benefit to them. Reward this valuable assistance with some additional added value or extra service. Then, when you have these testimonials, use them to establish the credibility, comfort and trust so essential to encourage people to open up their network of contacts to you. Good testimonials will pry open even the most stubborn doors.

Develop a Unique Selling Proposition (USP)

Develop a brief (10-second) statement that explains the benefits of what you do. What benefits do you deliver to your customers? Why do you do it better than anyone else? Practice this presentation continually until it is brief, snappy, and memorable—and then use it frequently. Repeat it often enough to your contacts and to the people you approach for referrals, and you'll find that your message starts to get recognized. Even use it when leaving voice-mail messages.

Thank You!

By now it must be standard practice for all effective marketers to send a simple "thank you" note to customers every time they do some more business with them. Do the same for those who refer business to you. Let them know how the referral worked out, how you looked after their contact, and how their recommendation has benefited their contact, them, and you. That way, they'll want to help you again.

Here's a Referral for You!

Who do you know that might be able to use products and services of your customers? What goes around, comes around. Business karma is one of the most powerful sources of ongoing referral business—Givers Gain!

When to Use Word-of-Mouth?

Use it *all the time!* When you close a sale, ask your new customer for the name of anyone else who might have the same problem or challenge that you were able to solve for him or her. Ask for referrals when you send a thank you for new business, or when you make support or service calls. Don't assume that because you asked once, your prospect or customer is now tuned in to your need for referrals—they may have just heard of a need for what you offer, but not made the connection

Put your words in as many mouths as possible— and your success will be on everyone's lips.

because it has been some time since you last reminded them. Even ask when you've finished outlining your products and services to a new prospect (whom you feel has been impressed by what you had to say). Make it a habit to seek referrals continually. Use your USP.

Happily for those who do recognize the value of word-of-mouth marketing, most businesspeople just don't get it. Take advantage of this opportunity. Put your words in as many mouths as possible, and your success will be on everyone's lips.

Strategy 14

Pass it On

Pass it On

Delegate for Success

If there were a single zero-cost initiative—one that could be implemented immediately, that would motivate your people, improve team morale, grow team skills appreciably, increase productivity and profit, reduce your stress level and free up your time—would you go for it?

There is such an initiative and, by the time you've finished reading this strategy, you'll have a plan in place to implement it for yourself. The secret is delegation.

Take out a pen and paper and follow these simple steps to quickly draw up a delegation plan—one that will allow you to maintain effective control of all your tasks while still delegating effectively.

Look at What You Can Delegate

Recurring or routine tasks are the obvious candidates for delegation. Draw up a list of all tasks you undertake on a regular basis. List them under three columns—Task Name, Time to Complete, and Special Skills. Mentally work through your week, hour-by-hour, day-by-day. If you need some reminders, pull out your planner or To Do lists and look for clues there. Or make a commitment to track yourself during the next week and record the tasks you undertake.

Then, review that list for suitability to delegation. Are there any tasks you used to do when you were in a more junior position? (If so, why isn't someone more junior doing them for you now?) Which of these tasks could be undertaken by absolutely anyone? Are there any tasks on the list that require special skills that are in greater abundance in your team than in you? All of these tasks are prospects for delegation. Now, draw a line through anything that is not a suitable candidate for delegation—besides the obvious, these include personal messages (i.e. collecting your dry-cleaning), HR issues like reviews or disciplinary matters, or management of crises (after all, you're paid to lead). What's left are tasks that you can delegate.

Plan Your Delegation

Draw up a brief description of each *delegable* task: why it's undertaken, how it's been done in the past, when it must begin, when it must be complete, and what the outcome must be upon successful completion. This last point is key— you must have clear goals for the task, goals that are defined in an absolutely unambiguous manner that will make them easily communicable. What specific results must the delegate achieve in completing the task? You know you have a successful task description if a stranger could pick up your description and understand what's required.

Decide Who to Delegate to

You can delegate to use an existing team-member's skill more effectively, or to develop new skills in a team member. Either match an individual's proven skills to the requirements to the task or match in terms of the particular skill growth that you want to see in any given team member.

The first thing your delegation candidates will ask (themselves) is *"What's in it for me?"* Identify why the task is important and how it contributes to the overall success of the group—people need to feel that what they are asked to do is truly meaningful. Then, determine what growth or development they will personally achieve from developing competence in completing this new task.

> To delegate successfully, you must have clear goals for delegated tasks.

Well done! You now have a delegation plan that you can begin to implement immediately. To put it in motion, you'll need to do the following.

Delegate Each Task

Don't do this in two minutes over coffee, or as you pass in the corridor. Accord the exercise the time necessary to explain the what, how, where, when and why of the task; what's in it for the team member who will take on the task; and how and when you will review progress and completion. Take time to *sell* the task and you'll motivate these individuals to successful completion. Demonstrate your confidence in the selected candidates, reassuring them that you will be there to provide support should the need arise. If the task is particularly challenging, provide the security of more frequent reviews, with clearly agreed milestones of the progress expected and agreed key points. This is essential to providing you with confidence that you still have control of tasks you've delegated.

Pass Ownership

Accountability without power is de-motivating. Pass the new delegate the necessary authority to complete all aspects of the new task without coming back to you. Be clear, however, in setting the upper and lower limits of this authority in a manner that leaves no room for misunderstandings.

Review the Delegation

When you delegate a task, you agree to specific review points. Be sure to undertake these reviews, providing advice and course correction as required. If there are problems, identify the root causes—is it lack of confidence, lack of skills, or something else? Work with the delegate to see how you can jointly address the difficulty. Encourage the delegate to come to you not just with difficulties, but also with his or her own ideas on how to overcome them. Don't be tempted to review progress more regularly than agreed, or to encourage "reverse delegation"—where the delegate is at your desk every five minutes asking what to do next.

Celebrate Success

When a delegated task is completed successfully, be sure to recognize the delegate's achievement—provide him or her with feedback and be sure that their success is known within the group.

Do it Again

Every so often, go back and review all of the tasks you're undertaking with a view to passing on as many of those tasks as you can. If you're paid to manage, then manage— don't do.

You don't have to spend money to get greater productivity and profitability, and to improve motivation, reduce your stress level and free up your time—you just have to delegate. *Pass it on.*

Strategy 15

Getting to Know You

Getting to Know You

Success is All About Relationships

Exceptional products and services, outstanding prices, and excellent service after the sale are no longer a guarantee that your best customers will stay with you. A loyal customer base can be established only through Customer Relationship Management—which requires the conscious focus of the entire company on the development of mutually profitable customer partnerships.

A Personal Story From Jim Sirbasku

One of the things about Profiles that make Bud and me especially proud is the number of wonderful relationships we have formed with so many people around the world. Bernard Rapoport, a former CEO of American Income Life, a large insurance company, is one of these people. One day, he mentioned he was looking for someone to conduct special training for his salespeople. Mr. Rapoport told me about the specific information he wanted to impart, and it happened to be a subject in which I consider myself something of an expert. I told him I would be delighted to speak to his salespeople.

Agents and managers from across the United States attended the company's next quarterly meeting. My presentation was well received and Mr. Rapoport reported that I received more favorable comments than any of the company's previous speakers. Because of this, I was invited to do the presentation at the company's next annual convention.

I continued to participate in the company's training at their home office as well as regional conferences around the country. During this period of time, I noticed that the company used more Profiles' assessments. In fact, after every one of my sessions, the number increased substantially. I feel our business was helped because I was able to form relationships with Mr. Rapoport's people. I spent a great deal of time with them and got to know their individual situations and specific problems. This knowledge made it possible for me to relate to the company's independent agents and managers on a very personal basis and learn about their business. I then made specific recommendations of Profiles' products to help them to increase their efficiency and sales. This is a typical "win–win situation." The company's agents and managers benefited from the information I provided, and Profiles capitalized on the increased business. All of this happened because of relationships. In business, building relationships builds sales!

Existing Customers—Your Greatest Assets

There are two ways to increase your sales volume:

- Find new customers, and

- Sell more to existing customers.

Most companies seem to focus naturally on the first option. Traditional sales training and methodologies historically have focused on selling new business, often to the detriment of the development of existing customers. The reality is, however, that it is usually less expensive, and consequently more profitable to sell more to an existing customer, than to win a new customer. Here's why.

It Costs Less to Sell to an Existing Customer

Selling new customers requires a courting period during which time you convince prospective customers to do business with your company. Once they're landed, and assuming that you do an exemplary job of meeting their requirements, selling them again and again, and more and more, becomes easier. Plus there's so much more the existing customer can do for your business.

Existing Customers Will Refer You

Whether they refer you to other divisions of their company, or to other companies, existing customers offer you a valuable source of potential revenue. Referrals generally come only from existing customers comfortable enough to stick their necks out and recommend you.

Existing Customers Will Pay More

Existing customers place a value, firstly, on the time they save in not having to re-educate suppliers about the basics of their organization's workings each and every time they need help, and, secondly, on the lesser risk that is attached to doing business with someone they know will address their requirements in a quality fashion, on time and within the budget. This is added value, for which we'll all gladly pay.

Seven Steps to Better Customer Relationships

Relationship development is something that is generally considered to be the sole responsibility of individual sales-people. Successful relationships are often considered dependent upon the personal abilities of salespeople to establish rapport with key individuals in important accounts. It shouldn't be so. Relationship building can be formally planned and monitored in exactly the same fashion as any sales or marketing campaign—by setting firm objectives for everyone who has any contact within the key customer accounts, and by measuring performance against those objectives. A relationship-development program should include action plans to realize the following objectives, at the very least.

> *Relationship building can be formally planned and monitored in exactly the same manner as any sales or marketing campaign.*

Involve Everyone

Make sure that all personnel who interface with customers: Know something about each customer's business...know the names of key contacts...understand the priorities of different customers in terms of the products/services they source from you...share the value that you place on your customers' priorities, and portray a partnership approach to addressing them...appreciate what makes your organization's products/services so special...and view complaints as a high priority and a chance to excel

However, involving frontline personnel is only half the task. Senior management must also take responsibility for working with account-development teams to establish peer-level contact in customer accounts. That sort of contact can open doors that would otherwise remain closed to sales or support personnel, and insulates the account relationship from dependence on a single contact, such as the salesperson.

Know Their Business Inside Out

Team members who have frequent contact within the customer account—sales or support people, for example—best build this level of customer knowledge. Customers will happily provide you with information that makes this awareness possible. Personnel in contact with the account should continually seek input through questions like:

- What are your organizational objectives—short, medium and long term?

- What are your department's objectives?

- What part will you play in meeting these objectives?

- How might the operation of the organization be improved?

- How might the operation of your department be improved?

- What do you view as the key trends in your industry?

- Whom do you consider to be your main competitors?

- How do you position yourself against these competitors?

Know Them Personally

People make decisions based on who they are. Account teams should seek to understand personal ambitions and objectives—where do their contacts see themselves going in the context of their organizations: What are they trying to achieve? Can your organization be an ally in helping them to meet their personal objectives or career aspirations? Harvey Mackay, a successful entrepreneur who has written several bestselling books, including *Swim with the Sharks*, has a system called the "Mackay 55"—containing at least 55 pieces of information on every one of his business contacts. The availability of inexpensive, easy-to-use, online customer retention systems, like Salesforce.com, makes the collection and management of this sort of information much easier than it has ever been. (You can test-drive this system free of charge for 30 days. Check it out at www.salesforce.com)

Pulse-Check the Relationship—Frequently

Account teams must take control of relationship development, continually seeking feedback about how you and your products/services are perceived. Be sure that they're not too afraid to hear what they're doing wrong, or too modest to hear what they're doing right, asking:

- Are we living up to your expectations?

- How can we improve what we're doing for you?

- Is there anything else we should be doing to ensure our position as a favored supplier?

- Is there anyone else within the organization to whom you feel we should be talking?

- Who is your number one supplier of (the same products/services your company provides)? Why?

- How can we become your number one supplier?

- Who is currently providing other products/services that we could potentially supply?

- Why are these suppliers used?

- What should we do to position ourselves for this business?

- What new challenges might we be able to help you to meet?

Account teams should listen to what they're told, and be seen to act upon it—feeding back any improvements or changes made as a result of customer comments.

Be Their Eyes and Ears

Another way to improve relationships with key account contacts is through the unsolicited provision of information that is relevant to their personal and organizational goals—identifying materials, ideas and news that might be of practical use to them. No one has as much time as they feel they need to keep up-to-date in today's fast-moving, information-rich business world. Sources include newspapers, industry periodicals and the World Wide Web. Maintain a steady stream of value-added communication with key account contacts. This alone can have a powerful effect in positioning you as a valued partner.

Thank Them—Every Time

It is not possible to overstate the impact of two such small words. Be sure that your customers are aware of the value you place on doing business with them.

Do it Again, and Again, and...

Make customer development an integral part of the way you do business. Ensure that everyone on your team understands the part they must play in maintaining and developing good profitable relationships with your major accounts. When almost every other aspect of your business environment is changing at a rate that makes even medium-term planning difficult, Customer Relationship Management provides a reliable link to a profitable future. Invest in it.

"Relationships of trust depend on our willingness to look not only to our own interests, but also the interests of others."
PETER FARQUHARSON

Strategy 16

Fast-Forward

Fast-Forward

When the Going Gets Tough

Deals are stalled, decisions slow in coming. That's when you find yourself in what appears to be a "slow motion" sales cycle. These are tough times, and they come around every so often. The only thing we can do about slow sales cycles is learn how to deal with them.

A Personal Story from Bud Haney

In our many years of doing business and associating with other people who own and manage businesses, Jim and I have noticed a tendency to regard certain times of the year as being periods of "slow business." I don't know how many times I've heard people say, "Well, business was down substantially last month—but it was August."

There's a tendency for people who are not in retail businesses to expect December to be a slow business month. The expectation is that most people are so involved with the holiday season that they don't have the time or the mental focus to pay attention to business.

The phenomenon known as "self-fulfilling prophecy" says that if you expect something bad to happen, it probably will. With that in mind, Jim and I decided years ago to use self-fulfilling prophecy in a positive way by countering the popular trends and expecting our business to get better when the majority opinion was that it was a slow time of year, or that business was trending downward.

112

We decided that since most people cut back on their activity in December, we would make a concerted effort to increase our activity. The result was that while others complained their business was off, we were able to maintain our momentum through the end of the year. We may not have done as well in December as in other months of the year, but we have always managed to keep December from becoming a sales disaster.

We carried this idea into our Profiles business and we have used the weekend following Thanksgiving to kick off sales campaigns, proclaiming, "December is the best month to sell Profiles' products!" The first time we used this campaign, we brainstormed every possible reason we could think of for December to be a great time to sell our assessments. Throughout the month, our salespeople were inundated with these ideas and urged to increase their activity. Many of them found that since the general trend is to cut back on activity, they actually had an easier time reaching people by phone and scheduling appointments. This concept gives our business a terrific boost and it should work for your company, too.

In a slow sales cycle, it's important to remember that your products and services are still as good as they ever were, or even better. At least some of your customers and prospects still have a clear need for what you sell, and they have the wherewithal to do business with you. You're still doing all the right things you always did to close business...but maybe you've got to do more of it, or you've got to do it differently.

A famous definition of insanity describes it as *"doing the same thing over and over again, but expecting a different result each time."* Tough times change the sales landscape. If you're still trying to sell the same people the same propositions as you did prior to a sales slump, you could just be a little crazy. It's time to stop and take a closer look at what exactly is going with your sales opportunities.

Before continuing investment of sales time and energy for uncertain return, give your sales funnel this three-step makeover and get your sales moving at full speed again.

> *Be very critical in qualifying the likelihood of deals in your funnel becoming real business.*

Step 1: Qualify Your Current Sales Forecast

Take a hard look at all of the opportunities on your current sales forecast—be ready to be very critical in qualifying their likelihood of becoming real business. Categorize every opportunity under one of these three headings:

1. *Business that Can Be Won in the Short-to-Medium Term if the Right Things are Done*

   These are the opportunities where there is still clearly a pressing need for what you've proposed, and the will and means to do business still exists.

2. *Deals that Look Doubtful Given the Recent Sales Slowdown*

Some of your opportunities will probably qualify as *"nice to have,"* as opposed to *"must have,"* in the minds of your prospect. In tighter times, these opportunities don't die—they just don't close; and the tantalizing prospect of bringing them home can tempt you into investing even more time and effort in something that won't produce anything for you in the short term. Be ruthless—regardless of how much time or effort you've already invested in these deals, be prepared to face the reality that they may not close for you until things start to look a little brighter.

3. *Dead Deals*

Bury them. Although it can be hard to walk away, you simply can't afford a time and energy investment in hopeless cases. Stop working on them; quit investing resources in them; stop even thinking about them. Save your time, energy and resources for less hopeless cases. Take them off your forecast.

Step 2: Look at the Purchase Process in Each Target Account

Now that you know which opportunities merit your fullest attention, you need to determine precisely what's going on in those accounts—what stands in the way of a decision in your favor? In good times, the power to make purchase decisions is spread far and wide within organizations, with many departments and individuals having independent spending authority. When things slow down, the decision-making process changes dramatically. The level at which purchase decisions are made moves up a peg or two (or three), and a greater element of centralized structure and control ensures that every purchase directly contributes to one of two primary goals—the reduction of costs or the increasing of revenues. Suddenly, previously "urgent" purchases are subjected to tremendous scrutiny at higher levels; and many just-about-to-close deals go into a sort of limbo where they neither close nor are lost—and the cashflow effects resulting from this are what mortally wound otherwise perfectly viable sales-oriented organizations.

Before you can do anything with your best opportunities, you need to understand the game you're now in—who else is now playing, and what new rules apply?

Your first port of call must be your current "champion(s)" or "buyer(s)"—that person or group of people who previously had the ability to say Yes! For a variety of reasons that include confusion and damaged egos, not all of your current buyers will be straight enough to tell you outright that things have changed dramatically and that they no longer hold the major sway over the decision-making process on your proposal.

There's a simple "litmus test" that will tell you whether things have changed or not. If you suddenly find that you can't get a direct answer regarding when your proposal will be accepted or rejected, where precisely it is in the decision-making process, or when a final decision will be made, then this unpredictability is likely coming from the fact that your buyer is no longer in control. And, if your buyer is no longer in control of the decision-making process, then your ability to affect the outcome has been seriously eroded. Think about it—if the decision is now being made a few steps further up the line, then for you to be successful, your former buyer must sell your proposition to the next level up, and so on, until it reaches the level at which a decision can be made. Continuing to sell solely to your previous buyer is more like Chinese Whispers than professional selling—you simply cannot be sure that your business case is going to make it up the line intact; you can't even be sure that your former positioning will even appeal to the new decision-makers.

> If you find that your current account contact can't tell you where your deal is in the decision-making process, it's likely that your buyer is no longer in real control.

The only realistic way to regain some control over the process is to identify where the decision will be made and by whom—and then to set about building bridges to that/those

117

person(s). Your current contact will be your best source of information on who is now involved in the decision-making process. But you need to be cautious—if the decision-making authority has passed from your contact's grasp, even to a degree, they may be feeling a little raw and disempowered. The last thing they'll want to do is help you to cut them out of the process. Remember, they too have had their plans disrupted and, if what you had proposed formed part of their plans, then you share common interests—even in the new buying environment. The first thing these former primary contacts will need is reassurance—that you'll help them to work through the internal sales process that has resulted from the decision-making responsibility floating further up the line.

You'll need a lot of information on any changes to the decision-making process before you can decide on how to proceed from this point. At a minimum, you must find out:

- Who will now have the final say on approval of your deal?

- Who else will be involved in the decision?

- What are their particular priorities (cost-cutting, revenue improvement, strategic positioning, etc)?

- What are the new priorities for the company as a whole? (You must know precisely what is motivating your new buyers to action and precisely what is fuelling their decision-making.)

- How is your proposal currently perceived (nice to have, must have, ho-hum...)?

- What, in the eyes of these new buyers, are the perceived risks of proceeding with your proposal?

- What are their alternatives and what are the relative benefits of those?

- What do your champions think you'll need to do to keep things on track? And how can you help (preparing business cases, providing presentational support, etc)?

With this information under your belt, you now know who you should be targeting—but with what? And before you rush off into selling to any newly identified buyers, be sure that what you have to offer is going to appeal.

Step 3: Examine Your Value Proposition

When the buyer or purchase process in one of your key opportunities changes, it's key that you see how what you have on offer stacks up to the expectations of the new buyers.

When you first submitted your proposal, the climate within the target organization may have been very different indeed. Previous arguments and justifications for your proposal may have become redundant—if they were not formulated to appeal to particular motivations of a new set of buyers.

With all of the understanding you have of the new decision-makers and their motivations, look critically at the business case you are currently promoting for your deal. Will it appeal to these new buyers with their different priorities?

You'll need to be convinced that your proposal stacks up under three main criteria:

Positioning

Be certain that all of your arguments and justifications will work two or three pegs higher up in the organization—it's key that you position your offering specifically to appeal to the motivations and objectives you've identified at this loftier decision-making level.

Financial Justification

In tough economic times, there is a greater focus on the basics—like cutting costs and increasing revenues. While the issues that will have sold your original contacts may well still be important, it will now also be key for you to quantify carefully the particular financial and strategic benefits that will accrue to them from implementation of your proposal. Almost all substantial purchases being made currently will be backed up by strong Return-On-Investment cases. Be sure that you have a strong financial justification that addresses what you now know to be the priorities of the now higher buyers.

Differentiation

Even if your newly constituted value proposition is well positioned and financially justifiable, you could still be exposed if it suffers any element of "me too"—if it is not sufficiently differentiated from the propositions of other competitors who may be vying for the same business. Don't forget your basic marketing—be sure that your proposition includes strong Unique Selling Propositions to put you head and shoulders above any potential competitors. Completely remodel your value proposition until you are satisfied that your "new" proposal will fly in the new decision-making environment.

Now Get Back Out and Start Selling Again

Only when you know what you need to sell, how best to position it, and who has to be sold, should you seek out your new buyers and begin the selling process anew.

Invest the time, energy and effort necessary to identify the potential winners in your sales pipeline; remodel your propositions to cope with changes in buying patterns; and watch your sales go *fast-forward*.

> *"My future starts when I wake up every morning... Every day I find something creative to do with my life."*
>
> MILES DAVIS
> (1926–1991)

Strategy 17

Buried Treasure

Buried Treasure

Who Knows What Treasure is Hidden Right Under Your Nose?

In the 1970s, the Dallas Cowboys football team adopted the philosophy of drafting the best athletes they could find, some of whom did not have any college football experience. In the process, they found genuine talent that everyone else in the National Football League had overlooked. However, in the long run, the Cowboys decided it was more productive to focus on drafting football players who had already proven themselves on the football field.

We see that many businesses have designed their selection process in a similar manner. They almost always hire good people, but they make a mistake of placing some of these people in positions for which they are ill suited. Perhaps you've heard someone say, "He looked good in uniform, but he couldn't play." That's a way of saying that an employee appeared to have all the attributes for success in a particular job, but didn't perform up to expectations. Everyone has hired and promoted people who turned out to be disappointments. The number of times we have heard about top salespeople who became lousy sales managers is painful. That mistake occurs because neither the company nor the employee has a clear understanding of what it takes to become an outstanding sales manager. Oh, for sure, the company has a job description in a file somewhere that the sales manager could dust off and read if he or she wanted to, but traditional job descriptions are inadequate today.

A complete job description goes beyond listing the duties that go with a job title. A complete job description has to describe the attributes of the person who will perform the job in an extraordinary manner because he or she has the right brain power, the right behavioral traits, and the right occupational interests for the job.

A Personal Story from Bud Haney

I used to think it was odd that Babe Ruth, considered by many as the greatest baseball player of all time, was never hired as a baseball manager. Now that I understand the importance of matching people with the work they do, I can see that the Babe's skills were totally unrelated to those needed to manage a baseball team successfully. At our urging, many of the companies that Jim and I have worked with will keep people who are failing in their jobs, but transfer them to different positions. Companies don't hire bad people, but they often put good people in the wrong jobs!

W e all subscribe to the idea that our people are among our greatest assets, recognizing that those organizations that stand head and shoulders above our peers and competitors in business tend to have superior people policies and, on the face of it, superior people. Accordingly, many of us spend a huge amount of time chasing the rainbow, at the end of which we know we'll find a pot full of those perfect people that our industry leaders seem to have, instead of focusing upon identifying the best in those who already make up our teams. And therein lies the secret of those organizations with people-based competitive advantage—it's not just that they identify and recruit great people (and, of course, that does help), but that they work with those people that they have to make them great—to find just what attributes they uniquely possess that can be developed and employed effectively within the organization, to build the sort of serious competitive advantage that only good people can confer.

8, 11, 15, 5, 14, 1, 7, 6, 10, 13, 3, 12, 2—what's the pattern in this series of numbers? Take a moment to look it over, and then, if you're stumped, turn quickly to end of this strategy for the answer. Then, read on.

So what? Well, the simple point is that sometimes looking at the familiar in an entirely different way can produce results that we scarcely expect. Your people are like that—you assume that because you've worked with them for a while, you know what they are, and what they're capable of. That's only true up to a point. To uncover genuine hidden potential requires a shift in the way you evaluate your people.

> *Successful organizations work with their existing people to make them world-class.*

Take the following actions to get you started.

Uncover Your Team's Career Goals, Aspirations, Likes/Dislikes and Strengths/Weaknesses

You can't begin this process without knowing a lot about each and every member of your team. Start by talking with them regularly. Find out what it is they like to do. Research published in a 1999 *Harvard Business Review* demonstrated that people excel at jobs that interest them deeply more than at jobs that their education, skills or experience might suggest are perfect fits for them. Find out what your people enjoy doing, what career plans each has, and where they aspire to go in your business or in life in general. Don't confine yourself to informal chats. Use more formal means like the *Profiles Checkpoint Multi-Rater System* (see www.profilesinternational.com) and psychometric assessments like the *Profile XT* to determine the particular strengths of your key assets. The authors of the *HBR* research cited above put it perfectly: "*...the best way to keep your stars is to know them better than they know themselves— and then use that information to customize the career of their dreams.*"

Make Better Use of Strengths

When you have a good appreciation of the particular strengths of each member of your team, start to look for new ways in which to apply them. Brainstorm on how you can apply these strengths in new or imaginative ways to enhance the roles of each of your people and to address problems that you haven't previously been able to address. In one successful example we observed recently in the IT industry, a talented project manager was put into the role of sales manager—not because she knew an awful lot about sales or had a gleaming sales record—quite the contrary—but because she was particularly good at organizing campaigns, marshalling resources, motivating her team to action, and seeing initiatives through to the end. Take off the blinders when it comes to applying strengths in new ways.

Turn Weaknesses into Strengths

In the movie, *Enemy of the State*, Gene Hackman tells Will Smith—"...in guerrilla warfare you gotta turn your strengths into weaknesses...if they're big and you're small, then you're fast and they're slow...you've got to work with what you've got." You've got to do the same with your people. Look at what you currently perceive as shortcomings, and then look at situations where those attributes could be positive—after all, most weaknesses are just overused strengths. For example, a Customer Service Representative who's just too assertive to "put up and shut up" with angry customers may actually make a very successful salesperson, capable of overcoming objections not easily overcome by others. Consider the marketing executive who comes up with killer campaigns but just can't seem to follow them through to the end—focus that person solely on developing the creative campaigns, and assign project management and completion to someone better suited. Look at every shortcoming you currently perceive in your team-members, determine where a weakness might become a strength, and figure out how you can capitalize upon it. You'll be amazed at the results.

Feedback, Feedback, Feedback

In a recent study, 25 percent of employees said lack of feedback from management about their performance was one of the main reasons for changing jobs. Make it a formal objective to provide positive feedback on a job well done to every one of your people at least weekly. This requires you and your management team to actively seek opportunities to provide feedback. Not only does this increase the interest level in the job being done (we all like to be recognized), but it helps to reinforce positive behavior and performance at the expense of more negative alternatives. Also, experience shows that when you provide feedback to your team, they'll provide feedback to you.

If you've been searching for a competitive advantage, then the answer may be just under your nose—before you start exploring more exotic sources, look at the people who are driving your company right now. You'll find untold treasure buried behind those familiar faces you see every day.

Pattern in the Numbers?

Being familiar with numbers and number-series puzzles, the natural inclination is to calculate the mathematical relationship between 8 and 11, and then between 11 and 15, and so on until you can speculate as to the mathematical progression—and there is none! The numbers are arranged alphabetically! Your people are so familiar to you, bur if you look at them a little differently, you can learn an awful lot more about what can make them great for you and your organization.

Thanks to Donna Engelson of Profiles National Capital for this teaser.

> *"Develop interest in life as you see it; in people, things, literature, music— the world is so rich, simply throbbing with rich treasures, beautiful souls and interesting people. Forget yourself."*
>
> HENRY MILLER
> (1891–1980)

Strategy 18

Death Valley

Death Valley

Cut Your Sales Cycle by Half

Would you like to save time, shorten your sales cycle, and close a larger percentage of first-time appointments? This sales technique requires no time or effort to implement, and it will dramatically improve your success rate.

First, let us take you back to a sales meeting from your past...you met a prospective customer for the first time on a Tuesday, and absolutely everything went as planned. You effectively engaged the prospect; everything "clicked" personally; your discovery process uncovered her needs clearly; and you discussed an outline solution that excited her. All in all, the call could not have gone better. You agreed with your enthused future customer that you would summarize the discussion in a proposal within days—and call to follow up a few days later. Sounds like the perfect meeting, doesn't it? Sounds like you got another sale!

You returned to the office, the clock now ticking. Since you didn't have a busy week, you started on the proposal on Wednesday, and you mailed it on Thursday. No point calling Friday—she wouldn't have had a chance to absorb the proposal yet, so you decided to wait until the next week.

The next Tuesday, you left your first voice mail. Several voice mails followed in the next few days. By Friday, now some ten days since your meeting, you breached the voice-mail defenses and actually got your prospect live. She had a "chance to glance through it but not really give it the attention it deserves" (you know she hasn't even looked at it yet but that's OK) and requested that you call early next week to follow up again.

Monday would look too desperate so you waited until Tuesday to call again...Another week went by. You finally got her on the phone again, and this time your once enthused prospect sounded anything but enthused. Nowhere near as enthused as when she suggested that you prepare the proposal! This time she told you she'd "*get back to you*"... and as time passed by, your prospect slipped away, never to be heard from again.

What happened? You fell into the biggest trap in sales. You wandered unwittingly into Death Valley—that dry zone that stretches from first contact to proposal follow-up. All around are the bleaching bones of the countless millions of salespeople who preceded you. Another thin-on-the-ground opportunity bites the dust.

> *Death Valley: that dry deadman's zone that stretches from first contact to proposal follow-up*

The conventional wisdom in selling suggests that this is an unavoidable consequence of selling—one of the elements in the "numbers game" that you just have to learn to swallow. *Not true!*

A Simple Solution

Make one simple change to your sales call right now and you can fix this problem forever. Every single time you meet a prospect, make the next appointment before you leave. That's it—simple but highly effective. Suppose it's your first appointment and you've agreed to prepare a proposal—don't leave without looking for an appointment to meet with the prospect again to bring the proposal back in to talk it through, within days if possible.

There are a couple of possible responses when you try to set the next appointment for a few days later.

1. The Prospect Agrees

You are already winning. For a start, you've qualified the prospect's interest. If he's prepared to meet you again, his interest looks genuine and you've immediately hacked a few weeks off your sales cycle. Also, your positive initial meeting won't have time to slip his mind.

When you next meet, he remembers why he was so enthusiastic about what you had to say, how you planned to meet his pressing requirements, and why he asked you to prepare a proposal. What salesperson wouldn't close more of those deals than the Death Valley specials above?

2. The Prospect Declines

"You know, the rest of my week is just completely full." You suggest early the following week, but "next week is even worse." She suggests that you "simply mail in your proposal." It seems now as though she doesn't want to solve the problem you recently discovered. Maybe you haven't uncovered her real issues and proposed a satisfactory solution. Or perhaps she's not the decision-maker. Or she doesn't have the budget. But even this is good news—because now you have information you didn't previously have. If you feel you've got the right person, right requirements, and an existing budget, then you can flip back into the discovery process and try to recover. If you've got the wrong person, then you can probe for the right one and start over. If it's simply a hopeless case, then slap yourself on the back—you just saved yourself the time, energy and effort, and the disappointment of eventually watching another one bite the dust! Now you can spend your time on more worthy prospects.

> Every single time you meet a prospect, make the next appointment before you leave.

You gain information, clarity and time when you ask for the next appointment during the current appointment. Implement this simple change to your sales process right away and soar over your competitors' bones in Death Valley.

"He who asks is a fool for five minutes, but he who does not ask remains a fool forever."

Strategy 19

Cold Comfort

Cold Comfort

Warm Up Your Cold Calls

Do you have a hundred-pound phone in your office? You probably do if you have to rely on cold calling. Or, if you've ever made cold calls in your past, you know what a hundred-pound phone feels like! It's so heavy you just can't pick it up to make those cold calls.

This "cold-call reluctance" generally stems from one of two main sources—fear of rejection or lack of preparation.

A Personal Story from Jim Sirbasku

As a neophyte in sales, I had great difficulty with cold calls. Lucky for me, my sales manager had dealt with the cold-call problem many times before and had a solution for me.

"Jim, do you find it difficult to call for appointments on the phone?" he asked me.

"No," I replied. "As long as I have enough referrals. But often I don't have enough of them."

Then he said to me, "Has it ever occurred to you that there are people who need your product more than you need to sell it to them?"

I was puzzled until he assigned me the task of listing the benefits to be gained from using the product I was selling. I thought of about ten things right away, and over the next couple of weeks expanded my list of benefits to about 25. Reviewing the list every morning gave me a reason to believe that the people I was calling would want to talk to me. That provided me with a degree of confidence and motivation that helped me overcome my fear of making cold calls.

But then my sales manager assigned me the task of making cold calls in the field for two days. I had to walk into a business, introduce myself, and attempt to schedule an appointment with a prospect. The purpose of the exercise was to convince me that it was a whole lot easier and more time-effective to schedule appointments using the telephone.

I quickly learned that the two most valuable assets I had were my time and my attitude! After two days of cold calling the hard way, I was convinced I could make more cold calls using the telephone. Plus, not having to drive all over town, park the car, find a prospect's office, and deal with the possibility of rejection in person improved my attitude! Not so amazingly, I had absolutely no trouble making cold calls on the telephone after that.

You'll Never be Rejected on a Cold Call

We all have fragile egos—to a greater or lesser extent. Nobody likes to be rejected. Anyone making cold calls needs to realize that the person on the far end of the phone has no idea who you are, whether you're pretty or ugly, tough or wimpy, nice or mean—they simply don't have enough information to

> *Anyone making cold calls must realize that the person on the end of the phone doesn't have enough information to reject them personally.*

reject you. So, when they cut the call short or don't respond to your pitch, they are rejecting what you're offering—and that's got nothing to do with you personally. Give yourself a break—shake it off. Remember that you are playing a numbers game, and every No gets you closer to your next Yes.

Anyway, if you were adequately prepared before making the call, then you know that that person could have benefited greatly from doing business with you—it's their loss. So there's nothing to beat yourself up about—unless you were unprepared.

The following tips will ensure you'll be so well prepared that cold-call reluctance will become a thing of the past.

What's in it for Me?

Everyone thinks, *"What's in it for me?"* Crystallize the particular benefits your product or service will bring to your prospects, and be so convinced by these benefits that you are anxious to share this information with anyone you can.

How will the prospect benefit from what you offer? How soon will these benefits be realized? What will it mean to them—will their businesses run better, sell more, provide better customer survive, reduce costs, or increase productivity? Why should they be excited by what you have to tell them? Once you know the answers to these questions, you'll find that you begin to want to make those calls—but don't rush off yet...

Know Precisely What You Want to Achieve Before You Make Any Call

Precisely what action do you want your target to take? Decide upon your primary objective for the call, and then set fall-back objectives. For example, your primary objective when you call might be to get an appointment to meet with them. Your first fall-back might be an agreement that you'll call again the following week to put the appointment in the diary, and a further fall-back that you'll call them to talk again once they have a chance to read some collateral you'll send by mail, or perhaps by e-mail. Be clear in what you want to achieve with every call you make—and have decided at what point you'll abandon one objective for the next desirable outcome.

Grab Their Interest Quickly

If you received a call from yourself, what would drive everything else from your mind long enough for you to tune in to the rest of the call? Come up with a statement or question that slaps your prospects in the face and makes them concentrate on what you have to say. For example, a colleague who works with a cell-phone operator boldly tells every financial director they speak with, *"We can cut your cellphone bills by more than 30 percent TODAY."* Grab their attention!

141

Ask Questions that Force Them to Think

Think of all of the primary benefits your prospects would get from doing business with you and ask questions related to these benefits that get them thinking. For example, *"How much would a 30 percent reduction in your cell-phone bills save you on a monthly basis?"* Engage them.

Get to the Point

Engage in conversation for only as long as it takes to hook your prospect's interest. Then ask for what you've called to get—be it an appointment, a sale, or whatever. Don't be drawn into longer conversations with those who hit it off with you on the phone—the longer the call, the more opportunity for rejection. Take only as long as it takes to get to the point where you feel your prospect is ready to move to the next step with you. Then bring the call to a close. Go for the gold early.

Get the First Call Over Quickly

The first call each day is the push that gets you going. If you have any way of grading your calls according to their likely success, start with the least important first—do your warm-up with your lesser prospects. Once the first is out of the way, things get a little easier—go straight into the second and work your way to the end of your call list. Get a rhythm and go with it.

Lighten your phone—be sure to prepare carefully any time you have to make cold calls, and give yourself a break when you get a No! Take comfort from the fact that there will always be some people too misguided to see how much you could have done for them.

Strategy 20

Examine Your Conscience

Examine Your Conscience

Repent! Ye Sales Sinners!

Failure to ask for the order more than once is the selling sin most difficult to overcome. In fact, we have observed salespeople who did not ask the first time. We have often told salespeople that if they get an order the first time they try to close, they should be amazed and surprised. Most buyers will say things like, "I need to think about it," or "Let me talk this over with my staff." You should expect that. But make it your policy to ignore the first stall. Be prepared to respond with a reason why the buyer should say Yes right away and ask for the order again. Ask for the order at least five times on every call. If you do, you will see your income double, triple or quadruple.

A Personal Story From Jim Sirbasku

The Boy Scouts have a special coin to remind the Scout to do his good deed for the day. Every morning, he puts the coin in the right pocket of his pants and moves it to his left pocket after he has done the good deed. A sales manager I once worked with taught me to use the same technique when closing sales.

I carried five quarters in my right pocket and moved one to the left pocket each time I asked a prospect to buy. One time, I became confused about the direction I was moving the quarters and I had asked the closing question eight or nine times. While I was passing one of the quarters, I dropped it on his carpet. The buyer had noticed my confusion and could tell I was doing something out of sight behind his desk. He stopped me in mid-sentence and asked me what the bleep I was doing.

I explained my system and apologized for losing track of how many times I had tried to close the sale. He good-humoredly suggested I stack my "closing quarters" on his desk so I could keep track of them and start again.

A little embarrassed, but happy he had not thrown me out of his office, I stacked the quarters as he had suggested. He looked at me expectantly so I asked the first of my new series of closing questions. At first, all I saw on his face was a big grin and then he began laughing and said, "OK, you win—I'll buy it!"

For businesspeople, everything revolves around sales. No sales, no business. When sales start to go off track, it is usually because we've committed one or other of the sales sins below. Do a quick decade of sales meditations and clear your conscience. Are you or your salespeople guilty of any of the following?

I. Forgetting that Sales is a Numbers Game

Research shows that most successful salespeople spend as little as one-third of their time selling. The other two-thirds are spent cultivating leads and prospects to ensure that they have plenty of selling opportunities available to them on an ongoing basis. Salespeople fail when the pipeline dries up.

Examine your conscience: *Am I working consistently hard to keep a constant flow of leads and prospects in the pipeline or am I relying on pot luck?*

2. Giving Up Too Early

A major study showed that:

- 48 percent of salespeople make one call and stop
- 25 percent make two calls and stop
- 15 percent make three calls and stop
- 12 percent go back and back and back and back.

Not surprisingly, the study also found that it is this latter 12 percent who make most of the sales!

Search your heart: *Do I ever give up too quickly?*

3. Making Friends, Not Prospects

The originators of relationship marketing and selling have a lot to answer for—it's so easy to justify the time you spend with people you like or people who like you. Don't fool yourself—the people you like are not always the best prospects and, while looking to develop good relationships with all of your contacts is laudable, much more important is clear focus upon

Spend your time with the best prospects—not the prospects you like best.

what each and every one of them will deliver to your bottom line.

Be honest: *Is it the value of prospective business or the warmth and comfort of a relationship that drives my interest in prospects?*

4. Talking More than the Prospect

The more your prospect talks, the more you learn. The more you learn, the better your chance of winning the business. The most successful salespeople facilitate a process whereby the customer becomes so involved in the sales process, they do most of the talking—the salesperson simply becomes a facilitator.

Tell the truth: *When I examine my sales calls, who's doing 95 percent of the talking?*

5. Not Learning the Prospect's Business

You can tell when the salesperson who is trying desperately to part you from your money has learned enough about your business to make a useful contribution to its development. Your prospects are no different. Fail to learn the prospect's business and, regardless of the super relationship you've built, the register rings "No Sale!"

Ponder: *Am I taking the time to learn my prospects' businesses?*

6. Not Winning the Customer's Confidence

Prospects don't completely believe in your public relations, advertising, or product promotions—they believe in people.

You are your product. Fail to win their confidence and you'll fail to sell. It's that simple.

Look into your soul: *Do I communicate an honest, professional, capable partner that my prospects can rely upon?*

7. Not Selling the Company

Even the most seasoned salesperson can sometimes forget that a convinced prospect will wonder what's behind the scenes, supporting the salesperson. They'll think: *"What happens to me if my sales rep is gone tomorrow?"* There are always three sales to be made—the products, the salesperson and the credibility and reliability of the company behind them.

Tell the truth: *Do I always focus on making all three sales—me, my products AND my company?*

8. Not Joining the Customer's Team

It's no longer enough to have high-quality products and services—everyone has those. Prospects today want knowledgeable, effective and consultative partners who will contribute some additional knowledge and expertise to their team. Helping customers directly to address business challenges is what makes the difference between peddler and consultant.

Meditate: *If I were gone tomorrow, would my customers miss my expertise in their business?*

9. Not Creating a "Benefits Vision" for the Customer

In order to buy, we all need to have a clear picture of the many benefits that will accrue to us from anything we purchase. The most successful salespeople work hard to build in the minds of their customers a clear, compelling vision of the benefits of everything they sell. This clear mental picture of a "happiest ever after" scenario is key to consistent sales success.

Search your heart: *Do my presentations evoke an emotional response—can my prospect clearly visualize the benefits of buying from me?*

10. Not Going that Extra Mile

All of us are at our best when we are on the brink of closing a deal with a prospect—especially the first deal. We'll all do our level best to ensure that we satisfy every one of our prospect's demands at this key stage. That's why no one is overly impressed by extra effort at sales time—it's the norm for you and for all of your competitors. What counts is how you behave when the sale is done. Do you deliver? Do you keep your promises? Do you live up to expectations by keeping promises and ensuring that your customer gets a return on whatever they buy from you? Are you still around delivering real business value between sales? If your follow through is poor, your follow-up sales will be, too.

Examine your conscience: *Am I known for consistent world-class follow through?*

Keep your conscience clear, your selling religiously free of these sales sins, and see your business soar to heavenly heights.

> *"Men are punished by their sins, not for them."*
> ELBERT HUBBARD
> (1856–1915)

Strategy 21

A Perfect Pitch...

A Perfect Pitch...

Creating the Perfect Pitch

Research shows that most people fear making a public presentation more than they fear death—the majority of funeral attendees would rather be in *the casket than* up *delivering the eulogy!*

That's because most of us have bought into the myth that "Good presenters are born, not made." *There are some people who have natural abilities that make presentations easier for them but, with a little help, anyone can become a competent presenter. To paraphrase Thomas Edison:* "Great presentations are 10 per cent inspiration and 90 per cent perspiration." *The perspiration in presentation is preparation, preparation, preparation.*

A Personal Story from Bud Haney

Throughout my years playing baseball, I would often study pitchers. Although my job was to be a hitter, I figured any knowledge of my opponent would give me an advantage. I discussed with the pitchers on my team the strategies they employed to get hitters out. The sum total of my research led me to believe that the key to pitching successfully is to find the most vulnerable spot in a hitter's swing and exploit it. If you know the opposing batter cannot hit a curveball, then throw him curveballs and let him get himself out. Each batter has a weakness and it must be found in order for an opponent to be successful.

On the other hand, each batter has a spot where they like the pitch to arrive. The perfect pitch is different for every batter. A salesperson can learn from this methodology.

Every potential customer has a pitch they find appealing. If you can deliver your pitch to the right spot, you allow the customer to hit a homerun. Unlike baseball, everybody wins when your customer connects.

Next time you have a presentation coming up, include these key steps in your preparation.

1. Don't Talk to Strangers

You haven't a hope of persuading an audience you don't know. You must know all you can about the members of your target audience. What are their backgrounds? What are their concerns? What will turn them on? What will turn them off? Where do they stand on the topic you're presenting? How much do they know about your topic? Know your audience inside out.

2. Begin with the End in Mind

Before you even think about preparing your killer presentation, you've got to clarify precisely what it is that you intend this presentation to achieve. You've got to ask yourself, "What do I want my audience to do when I've finished making my speech—and what will make them want to do that?" Expand that further to determine: What's my key message? What's in it for the audience? What are the benefits of what

I'm proposing to the audience? What might prevent them from taking my advice? What precise action do I want them to take as a result of my presentation, and when?

3. Structure Your Presentation

Before you run off to start up PowerPoint, be sure that you have a compelling structure on the ideas you plan to outline in your presentation. A *Problem–Analysis–Solution* approach will work for every presentation, and ensures that your presentation has a structure even the slowest member of your audience will be able to follow.

- First, Identify a Problem

  The problem is the issue that has you on your feet presenting. Identify the problem your audience needs solved. Maybe it's a problem they already recognize; but, more likely, you are setting out to provide them with a solution to a problem they haven't yet recognized—perhaps they need a new product or service to improve something they already do, or perhaps you need them to adopt a new marketing strategy to maximize their return on marketing investment. Whatever issue your presentation is addressing must be understood by every member of your audience right from the start. First, define the problem.

- Second, Analyze the Problem

  Now, use facts, figures and clear examples to explain the problem's background, why it exists, what impact it's having on the day-to-day lives of your audience, and why it needs to be addressed.

- Then, Provide a Solution

  If you've done a good job with the first two steps, your audience is waiting for you to provide a solution to the problem you've outlined and analyzed. Be sure that your solution is carefully formulated to address all of the issues raised in the previous two steps.

Base all of your presentations on this simple three-step process, and your audience will instinctively understand where you're going with your presentation and will easily go there with you.

4. Build Your Presentation

With the advent of effective and affordable software packages like PowerPoint, it has never been easier to build an attractive presentation. Be sure, however, that your PowerPoint software supports your presentation—and does not dominate it. Here are some general guidelines for the effective use of presentation software and other aids:

- Keep your slide content in brief bullets and try to keep to about four bullets per slide.

- Avoid the clip art that comes with your package—most people will have seen it already and will find it boringly familiar. If you must use clip art, source some more interesting images on one of the many websites dedicated to the subject.

- Be wary of animated titles or clip art—they can distract from the message.

- Leave out bullet-point sound effects like sirens, skidding tires, typing, laughing or applauding. They are distracting and amateurish.

> *Leave out fancy animations, sound effects, fancy fonts and wild colors— don't lose your message in your medium.*

- Use video clips only if they are good quality and add something to your presentation that you can add in no other way—again, they can tend to distract.

- Choose simple fonts and use basic, primary color schemes.

- Give your slides headlines, not titles. Use them to summarize the key message in each slide. For example, "Better staff recognition means greater retention" instead of "Staff Recognition Strategy."

- When you've finished with a slide, don't leave it on display—particularly if the discussion has moved on. Your audience will still sit there analyzing that slide instead of listening to you.

- Leave the gadgets in your desk—there's nothing a laser pointer can do that your hand can't do more effectively. And it's distracting—you'll get more inquiries about where you bought your pointer than about your presentation. Dump the laser.

5. Polish Your Presentation

Think you're finished? Not nearly! All you have now is the first draft—and that's what it will remain until you polish it. Before you set about polishing your presentation, revert back to the objectives you set for your presentation in Step 2—and think about the problem you set out to solve following the advice in Step 3 above. Now, with a clear view of your objectives for the presentation, review your first draft as follows:

1. The "So What?" Test

Look at every slide and every point you make. If any of them don't contribute positively to the objective of the presentation—if you suspect that your audience might think *"So what?"*—then cut it. Unnecessary points find their way into every presentation and only increase the burden on the audience. Be ruthless in your editing.

2. Does it Flow?

You have established a problem, analyzed it, and then suggested how you can solve it. Does your presentation run in a straight line through these three key milestones? If it goes off track, cut the detours. You've told your audience the problem you're going to solve—stick to the point and make it easy for them to follow you straight to your logical solution.

3. Are You Repeating Yourself?

Another common error is saying the same thing too many times. Sure, repetition can drive a point home. Just be sure that your presentation is not weighed down by confusing redundancies.

4. Supporting Facts

Have you included enough hard facts and figures to back up your key points? Opinions are valuable, but examples, facts and figures will drive your key points home more effectively.

Congratulations! You have just completed a tightly argued and compelling presentation. Next, we'll look at how you practice it to perfection, create a high-impact opening statement to make a great first impression, pace yourself, interact with your audience effectively, and handle difficult audience members.

Strategy 22

...Pitched Perfectly

...Pitched Perfectly

Perfecting Your Pitching

Once you have your presentation finished, the key to success is practice. This means running through the presentation as if in front of an audience, until you have it down to a fine art. At that point, it's time to bring in a coach. If it's a key presentation, get the help of a professional coach—the small investment in a professional's time will pay off big dividends in the end. If you don't have the time or money for a professional coach, run your presentation past several trusted colleagues who understand the audience and your objectives. Solicit feedback about how you can improve the impact of the presentation. Do not proceed with a presentation without running it past someone's critical eye—even if they don't know your business too well, they'll spot gaps and flaws that you would otherwise miss.

The First Four Minutes

A few years back, the book, *The First Four Minutes*, explained how salespeople have just 4 minutes to make or lose a sale. Their prospects unconsciously decide whether or not they'll consider buying from them in the first 4 minutes of the conversation. Fail to grab the prospect's attention positively in the first 4 minutes and it's all over. This is not the case with presentations. Instead of 4 minutes, you have *10 to 30 seconds*! All other things being equal, your opening comments are really what determine the success or failure of your presentation. Your first statements must be strong and clear, and must grab your audience's attention immediately—otherwise the rest of your presentation is lost.

Think of the primary message you want your presentation to convey and condense it into a brief, powerful opening. Make your opening statement truly startling—get them thinking. One of the most effective ways to open a presentation is to go straight into a true (or, at least, credible) story or parable that makes your major point. People like stories. Unless you are 100 percent confident that you can predict your audience's reaction, and unless you are comfortable, forget the age-old advice to begin with a joke or funny story. As openings for presentations, they fail more often than they succeed—leaving a truly lasting impression when they go down in flames. Invest as much time and effort as is necessary to develop an opening that grabs the audience immediately.

> You don't get a second chance to make a first impression—you have four minutes!

Finally, never start into your killer opening until you're sure you have everyone's attention and complete silence. Every audience can be settled with a patient and relaxed "*sssssshhhhh.*" It works every time. Use it.

Move Quickly, Speak Slowly

People become bored with presentations when their minds have time to wander between ideas. Keep the development and presentation of your ideas and arguments moving at a steady pace—get to your points quickly. However, while you want to keep the flow of ideas flowing snappily, be careful not to speak too quickly. If you run your words into one another, you'll lose the audience. When you practice and deliver your presentation, remember that what sounds to you like extremely slow delivery rarely is—it's almost impossible to speak too slowly in a pitch situation. If in doubt, slow your speech down, pausing briefly after every word. Use variations of pace, volume and tone, or even short silences to emphasize key points.

Interact With Your Audience

This is a real double-edged sword—dangerous but highly effective. Dangerous? The problem with involving your audience is that the audience can take control before you know it. Effective? Involve your audience and the presentation becomes theirs—if they help make your points, then they can more easily buy into them. Combine Dale Carnegie's advice to *"Get them saying 'Yes, Yes' immediately,"* with the lawyers' rule—*"Never ask a question you don't know the answer to"*—and you have an effective way of involving your audience in your presentation, without allowing them control over its direction. A simple way to include the audience is to ask them questions and encourage them to raise their hands to show their agreement or disagreement.

Be Sure to Expect Disagreement

No matter how good you are, or how well structured your arguments are, someone (almost always) will not agree with you or with something you said. Expect feedback from these people, especially if you invite questions.

When you are rehearsing your presentation, take note of any points likely to generate disagreement. Develop and practice positive responses to these points so you will be prepared.

Here are a few basic rules to help you during a disagreement with an audience-member. First, pause, and be seen to think and consider what is—at least to the questioner—an important issue. After a few moments, restate the questioner's issue, ensuring that you include the emotional content they put into their point—show that you understand and appreciate their point of view even if you don't necessarily agree with it. Then, disagree in an agreeable fashion. Deliver your prepared alternative view. Don't be argumentative or heated. Respond to the entire audience, not just to the questioner. Make a particular point of finishing by making eye contact with someone other than the questioner. Finally, don't ask, "Did I answer your question?" You're only encouraging an ongoing two-way conversation. Address the issue and move on.

The Best Way to Win an Argument

Never, ever get into an argument. Although you may not always be aware of it, in the eyes of your audience, you are an expert. To them, you'll often have a psychological advantage over someone who disagrees with you, and, if an argument develops, you begin slightly ahead. Unfortunately for you, most people will tend to take the side of the underdog in any argument—and this is rarely the well-prepared presenter. The best way to win an argument is to avoid it. Arguments with audience members are a lose–lose proposition—even if you win the battle, you lose the war.

Much of today's business depends upon a good presentation, so it's amazing how many presenters choose not to invest the little extra effort in turning a *ho-hum* into a *wow*! Follow this straightforward approach and hit perfect pitch—every time.

Strategy 23

Just Say, "No!"

Just Say, "No!"

Choose Your Battles Carefully

There never seems to be enough good deals around, with the result that when an opportunity raises its head, you automatically find yourself off and running, working hard to win the business—each and every time. It's a knee-jerk reaction. But what if the target business isn't suited to the profile of your company? What if you can't possibly win the business? Or what if winning that business is going to have some negative effect on an existing valued customer or project? What then?

A Personal Story from Bud Haney

I recall making a presentation to a company that had been using a competitive assessment for about 15 years. I quickly realized that anything I said which suggested they were using an inferior product might have the same effect as saying, "You're stupid." Since I wanted to make a sale, but I didn't want to insult them, I looked for another approach. Shifting gears, I asked several questions and discovered an area in which they were not using assessments. Because Profiles has a wide range of assessment products, I was quickly able to lead the discussion in a different direction, and interested the prospect in a product that would meet their needs, but did not conflict with the assessment they were already using. Fortunately, I didn't waste any time chasing an opportunity that might have been out of my reach.

Unless it becomes your standard practice to make a formal bid/no-bid decision on every opportunity you uncover, you will never have a reasonable way of controlling, and improving, the level of return you achieve on the investment you make in preparing and selling your business proposals. You must make a bid/no-bid decision every time, and not be afraid to say No when circumstances demand it.

Why Bother with a Bid/No-Bid Decision?

Every deal you chase, win or lose, costs you in a number of obvious ways, as well as in ways you may not have considered.

Financial Costs

These are obvious—all of the costs associated with proposal preparation (time costs consumables costs, etc.) are marketing costs, and are just as real as those associated with advertising, public relations, brochure production, mailing and so on. Think of the time you will have to spend before you commit to spending on any of these more obvious marketing expenses—shouldn't you think carefully before jumping in and chasing every opportunity that comes your way?

Less Obvious Costs

What about the less obvious, less tangible costs of chasing unsuitable business?

Run a bid/no-bid analysis on every major opportunity that comes your way—it will save you time, money and heartache.

- Opportunity Cost

  What other, more profitable business might you have won and delivered if you weren't wasting your time on unsuitable deal opportunities?

- Confidence Cost

  How does the team feel if it loses deal after deal, even if it's because the opportunity wasn't really suitable? Unnecessary lost deals hurt team morale and drive.

- Profile Cost

  How does it look to the market when you chase multiple opportunities and win only a small percentage? How does it look if you pursue every opportunity that comes your way—what positioning message does it send about your business?

How Do You Make the Bid/No-Bid Decision?

Analyze every opportunity using the following straightforward three-step procedure:

1. *Use a Bid/No-Bid Questionnaire to Qualify an Opportunity*

   Be satisfied that every opportunity tests well on every count before even considering investing in pursuing it. Your questionnaire should include at least the following questions:

   - Where has the opportunity come from?

   - Are we technically capable of doing the work?

   - Will we need extra resources (people or equipment, etc.) to complete this work, and can we recover these costs?

- Is this our kind of work? Does it send the right message to existing and prospective customers?

- Do we want this work/ customer? Will it help to put our company "on the map?"

- Who is our competition on this deal? Can we beat them?

- If we win, how will this affect current business commitments?

- In landing this deal, might we lose or upset an existing, valued customer or some other prospective business?

- Could we achieve a better return on our investment of time, effort and cost in preparing this proposal if we focused our energies on other opportunities?

- Is the opportunity "rigged" for some other supplier? Are we just "making up the numbers?"

- Is this a "decoy" opportunity—formulated by the prospect to get some free research/consultation, or to help build a specification for a project to be undertaken in-house?

- Is there a definite budget for this project?

- What is the prospect's payment/credit record? Can we afford to do business with them?

2. *Your Proposed Solution Must Include a Unique Selling Proposition (USP)*

For those unfamiliar with the concept, a USP describes your product or service (your solution) in a unique manner. Avis has one of the most memorable USPs: "We try harder." Save your efforts for proposals where you can include a strong USP.

3. *Before Making a No-Bid Decision, Be Sure there are No Extraordinary Reasons to Proceed*

There will be deals you will decide to pursue even though the testing described above suggests they are unsuitable or un-winnable. You might decide to go after them for a variety of good reasons. For example:

- To Stay on the List

   Be careful, though—a poorly prepared proposal which obviously was not submitted to win, or which does not display your customary attention to detail, may be worse than no proposal at all.

- Learning Curve

   You may feel that the opportunity to learn how the prospect's business ticks and how best to approach such a customer may be of use to you in pursuing other players in the same sector.

- Positioning/Profiling

   Perhaps your strategic marketing positioning is such that you cannot be seen not to bid, or maybe you simply want to raise your profile in the target customer's organization.

The Bottom Line

In the end, the bid/no-bid decision-making process can be reduced to four basic questions that you should use to test all opportunities:

- Is this opportunity real?

- Can we win the business?

- If we do win, will it be worthwhile?

- If we can't win the business, is there another reason to bid?

Consider these questions every time you consider an opportunity and you will take control of your proposal hit rate. But when the process tells you that an opportunity is simply not right for you, say, "No, but thank you."

> *"Some have been thought brave because they were afraid to run away."*
>
> THOMAS FULLER
> (1654–1734)

Strategy 24

Look into the Future

Look into the Future

Are You on Track?

If you don't keep score in business and in sales, it may be hard to tell whether you're winning or losing.

A Personal Story from Bud Haney

Occasionally, I've skulked into Jim's office and said, "It's time for a 'William Wallace'." If you've seen the movie *Braveheart,* then you know about William Wallace. He's the simple farmer who inspired his fellow Scots to revolt against the powerful British who occupied the Scottish hillsides. Against all odds, Wallace led his countrymen to freedom, through his words and actions.

We rely on a "William Wallace" to give our salespeople a shot of adrenaline when we sense that they are getting complacent, or when our sales figures aren't meeting our expectations. We always operate with three sets of goals: a minimum goal, a realistic goal, and a dream goal. Because we're both aggressive, we more or less forget about the minimum and realistic goals and we go for the dream goal. We check the numbers daily to see if we are tracking toward the dream goal, and, if we fall a bit behind, we act quickly to get back on course.

Throughout our years together, I have seen Jim inspire our troops in astonishing fashion. I've seen him lift the spirits of people when they were down, shake up people when they became complacent, and motivate salespeople to aspire to unbelievable goals and then go out and achieve them.

A "William Wallace" amounts to a staff meeting where, frankly, Jim gets a little maniacal in front of our salespeople, arms flailing, ranting about how we have to do something to get our sales up. Let me tell you, when it comes to acting maniacal, Jim could win an Academy Award. The purpose is to get everybody fired up, to get them to refocus on their goals, and, ultimately, to go blasting toward our dream goal.

Even when we're making money, Jim can make it sound like the end of the world is near. His act never fails to get everyone's activity level up two or three notches. If our numbers aren't tracking the way we want them to—that is, if they're not going to lead us to our dream goal—then it's time to take action.

Whether you use the "William Wallace" method or some other action to keep your business on track, what's important is that you do measure.

Examine your conscience—have you ever prepared a sales forecast that ultimately didn't pan out? Anyone who tells you they haven't is either delusional or is riding a wave of so-far lucky statistics towards a fall. Even in good years, where sufficient revenues are achieved, the majority of sales forecasts are poor predictors of what is ultimately sold, when and to whom—but if we hit our numbers, it no longer matters, right?

Maybe in former years it didn't, but not in the new economy. No longer can any of us afford the luxury of a forecast that is not absolutely airtight—a truly reliable predictor of the outcome of all of the time, money and effort we plan investing in our businesses. So don't take chances. Review your sales forecast for reality—while there's still time to do something about any chinks you find in your armor.

Let's assume that your forecast consists of sales into existing and new accounts—sales you hope you'll make from beating the bushes for suspects, and sales already in process to some extent or other. In this strategy, we'll look at new business sales; later, we'll come back to reality, checking sales that have already made it from your suspect to your prospect list.

Let's begin a four-question reality check of your new business forecast.

Question 1: What are Your Projected Sales?

Look at the total figure you are projecting in sales from these yet-to-be customers. Now, consider what mix of products/services you project you'll sell into each of these accounts, and for what margin. Be conservative— don't project every new sale at the levels of the largest new sale you've ever made. Be realistic. Once you've worked this out, divide the value of your average new sale into your total target to get the number of new customers you're going to need to come in to finish on forecast. Great—now you have a clear picture of your targets for new customers, product mix and revenue/ margin figures. Hold those thoughts.

Before asking Question 2, look at your sales cycle. For the purposes of this discussion, assume you get your business from quotations or proposals. These quotations/proposals come about as a result of one or a series one-on-one meetings and/or presentations. Your one-on-ones are a result of initial appointments generated from lead-generation activity, and your primary source of lead generation is either cold or warm calls. If your deal cycle is different, then simply apply the thinking we're going to explore to the milestones that characterize your typical sale.

From Question 1 you know the number of new deals you need to close to hit the new business figure for this year. What are you doing about closing them? If you're not investing in enough focused activity, then, regardless of how desirable or possible the result you've projected, you just won't hit your numbers. But how can you tell if you're involved in enough of the right activity to assure your success? That's the focus of Question 2.

Question 2: What's Your Proposal Hit Rate?

Before you can determine the likely effectiveness of your activity plan, you need to do some research. Look into your past experience of your typical sales cycle to fine-tune your forecast. The first thing you'll need to estimate is how many proposals (based on your experience) you'll

have to produce to hit the number of deals you've forecast. If you don't have useful previous performance figures, then estimate conservatively—err on the side of more rather than fewer proposals. Let's say you get a 1-in-3 hit rate with your proposals. Then, to close 10 deals, you'll need requests for 30 proposals.

Question 3: How Many Meetings to Get to Proposal?

These proposals resulted from one or a series of meetings/presentations and selling activity. What does your previous performance tell you about the number of prospects you need to engage in one or a series of one-on-ones to get one prospect to the proposal stage? How many brand-new suspects do you have to meet before you find one that has an identifiable need for what you offer, and the budget, wherewithal and willingness to get a proposal from you? Again, conservative realism is key. If 1 of 2 contacts you meet results in a request for proposal, then your target of 30 proposals demands that you meet at least 60 new people.

Question 4: How Many Calls to Get a Meeting?

We assumed that you won these meetings from targeted cold or warm calls to suspects identified from your research. How many calls will you need to make? Let's say you have a 1-in-4 hit rate converting calls to appointments. To get 60 appointments, you'll need to speak with 240 new prospects. Finally, let's say it takes an average of four calls to get each of your target suspects on the telephone after you've mailed them. You have 960 calls to make this year!

In our example, your modest target of ten new deals demands that you:

- Make 960 calls to speak with 240 new people...

- to get meetings with 60...

- to get to the proposal stage with 30...

- to close 10.

When you work out your own forecast, it will uncover the reality of the work before you. If this were your forecast, assuming an even spread of activity over a 250-day business year, you'd need to make about 20 calls to new people per week; meet a new suspect every four days; dispatch a proposal about every eight business days; and close a deal every five weeks. These hard measures are the only objective means to determine the reality of your forecast.

You must know: How many proposals to get one sale? How many meetings to get to a proposal? How many calls to get a meeting?

Given where you are right now, how are you doing? Are you hitting your call, meeting, proposal and close targets so far this year? Be honest—if you're not meeting those targets, then it's back to the drawing board.

An in-depth look at your forecast will sometimes tell you that you simply don't have the time or resources to undertake the necessary activity. If the activity level required to hit your numbers is simply impossible, given other commitments like existing account selling, implementation, servicing or any other responsibilities you might have, then you cannot hit your forecast numbers without making changes. Do what needs to be done to hit the key milestones, and do it now!

If it's obvious you won't be able to hit your originally forecasted numbers, do something about any mis-projection now. You'll never have more of your year left than you do today!

The message is simple—take a hard look at your forecast for new business, and reduce it using a set of SMART (*Specific, Measurable, Achievable, Realistic, Timebound*) activity/ result milestones that allow you to determine whether you are on or off target. Make your forecast a living tool that ensures your success by comparing your actual progress against each of these milestones on a daily, weekly, monthly and quarterly basis—and adjust your course if you start to slide off target. Success or failure in sales does not happen by accident—the future is entirely in your hands.

Strategy 25

Back to the Future

Back to the Future

How Much is Your
Pipeline Really Worth?

How is it you manage to miss sales targets despite the fact that you always seem to have more than enough business any time you look?

In Strategy 24, we looked at how you plan enough of the right activity to be sure you have a fighting chance of hitting the aggressive sales targets you set yourself. Now let's take a look at how you manage the prospects that result from this ongoing activity—to be sure you have enough potential business at any time to keep you on your weekly, monthly and quarterly targets right to the end of a successful year.

To do this, you'll need to take three steps to establish structured forecasts that will operate as your early-warning system any time you begin to veer off target.

Step 1. Look at Your Deal Cycle

Map out your typical sales cycle and estimate how close each step in the cycle takes you to issuing an invoice. For example, we must meet 50 new people to get to the proposal stage with just 20 of them. Ten of these proposals will get a positive reception, and, of these 10, we'll eventually get a verbal Yes! from 6. Sadly, 1 of the 6 verbal go-aheads will fail to become new business—but at least we end up with 5 deals. The probability of closing a deal at each of the key points in our deal cycle is therefore:

First Meeting: *10% (5 in 50 become business)*

Issue Proposal: *25% (5 in 20 become business)*

Positive Proposal Presentation: *50% (5 in 10 become business)*

Verbal Yes: *80%+ (5 in 6 become business)*

Signed Contract: *100% (5 in 5 become business)*

If you don't have historical data to estimate conversion rates at each stage, start collecting data for future use, and, in the meantime, estimate working percentages cautiously.

Step 2. Estimate the Real Value of Your Prospect List

Consider the prospective sales you're currently working on—what are they really worth? Regardless of how good you are, some of those deals will close, and some won't. The chart below helps you to calculate the real value of your current prospects.

Prospect	Potential Value	Probability	Real Value	Close Month
Profiles	$20,000	25%	$4,000	June
Strategy	$15,000	50%	$7,500	May
CustomerCo	$10,000	80%	$8,000	April
Total Forecast			**$19,500**	

From the discussion in Step 1, we know that if we issue 4 proposals, we end up with at least 1 deal; so any 1 proposal is worth just 25 percent of its potential value. Having issued Profiles with a proposal, we estimate its current real value as 25 percent of the total $20,000 of the proposal. With Strategy, we've had a positive reaction to our proposal presentation, and since we know that we tend to close about half

> *Be honest: how much is your forecasted business worth in real terms?*

of the deals that get to this stage, we've calculated its real value as 50 percent of the proposal value. Finally, CustomerCo has said Yes, but we're still awaiting a formal contract—we know that we lose 1 in 6 of the deals that get to this stage, so the value of that deal is just 80 percent of the proposal's value—it won't become a certain billing opportunity until we get a signed contract.

While there is potential for as much as $45,000 worth of business in our pipeline, the real value of our forecasted sales is just a fraction of this number.

If your target for a given quarter was $30,000, and the chart above was your quarterly forecast, then, before your analysis, you might have relaxed on the basis that you had 1.5 times your target in the pipeline! However, you now know that the total forecast has a real value well short of your target for the quarter—so you're going to have to get a few more deals into the pipeline to ensure that you will hit your numbers.

To manage your sales pipeline effectively, this analysis must be undertaken on a rolling basis. That way you will always know which activities you need to engage to hit your targets.

Step 3. Look at Your Timescales

The last column in the above chart contains information on your forecast that is frequently most difficult to get right—

the estimated timing of closing each deal. Both salespeople and customers tend to overestimate how quickly they'll get to a Yes. If in doubt, be cautious. When you get this element correct, your forecast becomes even more useful. Now, you can reorganize your analysis in the manner of the chart below:

Prospect	April	May	June
Profiles	—	—	$4,000
Strategy	—	$7,500	—
CustomerCo	$8,000	—	—
Totals	**$8,000**	**$7,500**	**$4,000**

This analysis shows the trends that will affect your sales over the coming months. In the above example, it is clear that sales are tailing off over the three months of the quarter. To remedy this slippage, it's clear that some of the activity scheduled using the approach discussed in

Strategy 24 may have to be accelerated if sales are not to disappear altogether by the next quarter.

Ongoing analysis will provide you with all of the information you need to ensure achievement of even the most aggressive sales targets. Open up your own window on the future today and eliminate the element of chance from achievement of even the most aggressive sales targets.

Strategy 26

Sales Doctor

Sales Doctor

What Ails your Sales?

In the process of working with thousands of salespeople to help them sell more and increase their incomes, it has been readily apparent that most salespeople, when they have a selling problem, have difficulty objectively analyzing their situations and doing something about it.

A Personal Story From Jim Sirbasku

Many years ago, I discovered a method for pinpointing specific sales problems, called the Sales Doctor Flow Chart (see chart below). It is easy to use and quickly gets to the core of any sales problem. I remember working with an insurance agent who had about 25 salespeople on his staff. I showed him this method for identifying sales problems and, within six months, his people had more than doubled their production.

Ann, a young woman on the agent's sales team, was a hard worker, had many appointments, but did not close many sales. We sat down with her to analyze the reasons for her below-average productivity. By tracing her situation along the Sales Doctor Flow Chart, we moved along the chart until we diagnosed the situation as "Not Closing."

I asked her to pretend I was a prospect and that she had just given me her best presentation. Then I had her demonstrate her closing technique. Ann was good! She was so good, I almost bought a policy. Referring back to the flow chart, we decided to explore the area of "Poor-Quality Prospects." Her boss had commented on her effectiveness in getting appointments on the phone. That comment, along with our diagnosis that she was probably calling on people who were not very good prospects, led me to the solution of her problem.

Working together, Ann, her boss, and I rewrote the scripts she was using to get appointments. We focused on helping her set appointments with legitimate prospects and not suspects. When I checked back three months later, Ann told me it was no longer as easy to get appointments on the phone, but because she was investing her time only with those prospects who wanted to talk about insurance, her business and her income had increased substantially!

I could give you many, many more examples of how the Sales Doctor Flow Chart has helped diagnose specific sales problems, but I've always enjoyed telling people about this example because it was unusual.

Are you selling as much as you should? Sales are the lifeblood of every organization—without sales, organizations wither and die. If you or one of your salespeople falls off track, use this systematic diagnosis to identify where you need to focus your time, money and effort to get back on track.

What Causes Low Sales?

As illustrated by the Sales Doctor Flow Chart, there are two basic problems. Either you're not getting in front of enough people or you're not getting to Yes! Which is it in your situation? Be honest, and then move down the chart to either *1. Too Few Presentations* or *2. Not Closing*.

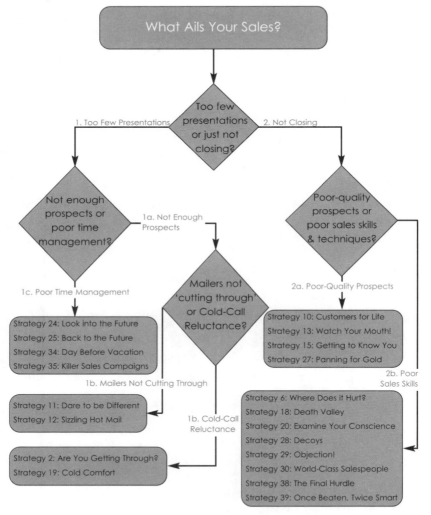

1. Too Few Presentations

There are two main reasons why salespeople don't get enough one-on-one meetings. Is your problem that you

1a. Can't Generate Enough Prospects or is it *1c. Poor Time Management*, and therefore you cannot get face-to-face with enough prospects? Decide where your stumbling block lies and then continue.

1a. Can't Generate Enough Prospects

If the problem is one of a prospect drought, you need to act urgently—once your prospect pipeline dries up, you are living on borrowed time. Look at your sales targets and determine how many units of your products or services you need to sell to make your target. Then, determine how many proposals it takes to get a sale, how many meetings to get to a proposal, and how many telephone conversations or mailers you need to get a meeting. Divide these activity targets by the selling days in your business year. If you haven't created and implemented a solid plan to hit each of these activity targets reliably, you haven't a hope. Get your plan in place now.

If prospect activity levels are not your problem, consider other problems like *1b. Mailer Cut-Through & Cold-Call Reluctance* or *2b. Poor Sales Skills & Techniques*.

1b.Mailer Cut-Through & Cold-Call Reluctance

Assuming you have a tight prospecting activity plan, and you know who you need to target with what, but you still have problems with too few prospects, then, either:

- Your mailers are not "cutting through," or

- You could be suffering from Cold-Call Reluctance.

Mailer "Cut-Through"

The volume of junk mail we all have to deal with rises daily and, unless your mailer is good enough, all of your effort goes straight in the trash. Don't panic—there's help at hand. Look at the Sales Doctor Flow Chart for advice on three strategies that can help you to turn all of your mailers into *sizzlers* that cut through to your prospect's attention every time.

> *Cold-Call Reluctance is a normal part of life for anyone involved in selling—and it's manageable.*

Cold-Call Reluctance

If your mailers are fine, but the follow-up a little slow, you may be suffering from the most persistent and corrosive of sales problems—*Cold-Call Reluctance*. Every salesperson has been afflicted with it at some time or other (regardless of what they might tell you!) *Cold-Call Reluctance* is exactly what it sounds like—a difficulty in picking up the phone to ask for an appointment or sale. All of the research in this area shows that call reluctance is fundamentally rooted in fear of failure. It can be addressed with training, coaching, and support. Before rushing into training expense, check out the Sales Doctor Flow Chart for two great strategies that address this sales killer.

1c. Poor Time Management

Some people are naturals when it comes to making the most of this basic resource—the rest of us have to use structured systems. Successful salespeople use systems for both advanced sales planning and day-to-day time management. The Sales Doctor Flow Chart suggests three great strategies to help you out with sales planning and forecasting—getting the Big Picture right. Your only remaining challenge is to manage your day-to-day activities to ensure that you execute your plan effectively. If you are not a natural time manager, invest in good-quality training from one of the many masters in this field.

2. Not Closing

Why do you sometimes fail to close after spending so much time to get in front of a prospect? Decide if it's *2a. Poor-Quality Prospects* or *2b. Poor Sales Skills & Techniques*, and then skip to that point and continue reading.

2a. Poor-Quality Prospects

Failure to identify and target appropriate prospects is one of the most basic sales ailments. There are four strategies to help you in these key areas. Check out the Sales Doctor Flow Chart to see which ones you need most.

2b. Poor Sales Skills & Techniques

So you're making lots of appointments with good-quality prospects but still not managing to bring in sales? If you don't have a clear structure to guide you from first contact through analysis of customer requirements and identification of benefits to a clean deal close, you need to fix that now.

The Sales Doctor Flow Chart provides you with eight meaty strategies which offer powerful and practical advice on these key sales skills.

The moment you see your sales start to suffer, Doc, use the Sales Doctor Flow Chart to diagnose the problem precisely and address it before it becomes an epidemic that wipes you out.

Strategy 27

Panning for Gold

Panning for Gold

Prospecting is a Lot Like
Panning for Gold

A Personal Story from Bud Haney

One day, we received a call from a big and influential consulting firm that was familiar with our product, and they expressed an interest in forming a joint venture with us. Jim and I decided this was a big enough opportunity that we needed to visit these fellows face-to-face.

A few days later, we met with several of the company's top executives, and, while we were talking, I commented on the great job their company did in finding new prospects. I said, "I guess the advertising you do must be paying off."

The executive who coordinates with the company's advertising agency told us, "To tell you the truth, those ads are really aimed at the clients we already have. They see our company on TV and it helps to keep us in the front of their minds."

"Oh," he continued. "It does help us get some new business, but we have another system for making sure we have all the prospects we need."

He explained that they keep a list of 1,500 prospects that they want to do business with and, in the fourth quarter of their fiscal year, they do extensive research and plan for aggressively going after business from these 1,500 people! While they don't get them all, their track record shows that they annually pick up several hundred new clients and increase their revenues from $2 billion to $4 billion annually!

I asked another question: "Do you mean you don't do traditional prospecting?"

"Our prospect list is the Fortune 500," was the answer. While the company consults with many smaller firms that usually contact them, this executive explained that nothing deters them from keeping their focus on the 1,500 prospects that make up their primary marketing target. What happens to the prospects they miss? They just carry them forward into the next year and try to figure out a better strategy for selling them.

We were impressed. We learned a lesson that day!

Prospecting for new customers is a lot like panning for gold. Know what you're looking for, look in the right places, use the right tools and techniques, and you'll get gold; otherwise, all you get is a worthless pile of well-sifted dirt.

It's hard to believe people who tell you they enjoy prospecting. Prospecting is a tough, time-consuming, and often boringly repetitive activity, fraught with ego-crushing rejection. But it's necessary. If you have a six-month sales cycle, you made the opportunity for today's sale six months ago. So your sales six months from now are entirely dependent on what you do today. Prospecting must be part of your everyday activities.

What most prospectors often miss is that the success of a prospecting campaign is determined before it begins. Two preparatory steps are vital.

Step 1. Develop a Formal Profile of your Ideal Customer

Forget about who you would like to be your ideal customer, or who your marketing or product people say are the ideal customers for your products or services. Look at who is actually buying from you, and who is buying from your closest competitors. *Who are they? What size are they? When do they buy? Why do they buy?* Draw up a formal profile of those customers—because you want to uncover more of them when you go prospecting. Summarize the profile so that you can recite it in 30 seconds or less—and be sure that everyone in your organization is equally familiar with it.

> Look carefully at the types of customers who are buying from you—know them inside out.

Step 2. Develop a "Why Us?" Statement

Prospects must have compelling reasons to buy from you. Develop a statement summarizing all of those reasons. In developing this statement, think: *What's so special about what I offer? How are my offerings superior to everyone else's? Who are my most impressive customers and why did they buy from me? What are my offerings' disadvantages and how can I overcome them?* Don't rely on yourself—ask your best customers why they bought from you; and listen carefully. Use this input to produce a conversational 30-second statement summarizing all of the reasons why prospects should buy from you. Refine it by reciting it to colleagues. When it's perfect, be sure that everyone who has contact with your customer or prospect base can produce it as required.

With a profile of your ideal customer, and knowing why they should buy from you, you are ready to start prospecting. *But only then.* Here are some guidelines that will make your prospecting activity less time-consuming and more productive.

Recognize that Prospecting is Not Selling per se

It is relationship building— creating an environment where a prospect wants to become a customer. Focus on the relationship—think of their needs, not yours. When the relationship is established, the sales follow.

> Prospecting is relationship building— creating an environment where a prospect wants to become a customer.

Keep Close to Existing Customers

Taking proper care of existing customers provides the easiest prospecting territory. Understand your sales cycle and be alert to when they should be repurchasing, upgrading or replacing. In larger accounts, prospect in new areas, using your knowledge of their business as a door opener.

Every Time You Sell, Look for Referrals

New customers are as positive about you as they'll ever be just after you've sold to them. Ask for referrals at the moment of sale. If they can't point you at anyone specific, find out how folks in their industry get information—i.e. trade associations, publications, websites, conferences, etc. Others like them will flock there.

Make Sure You're Visible to Likely Prospects

Find out what industry journals your prospects read and look at what they publish. Submit your own articles. Be sure that you know who organizes any regular industry conferences or events, and get yourself on speakers' lists. Make yourself a visible authority in your prospects' industries.

Network

Attend any forum, conference, exhibition or event where you know that your prospects will congregate. Talk to as many people as you can. Deliver your "Why us?" statement, exchange business cards, and move on.

Extend Your Reach

Lift a rock in your garden and you'll see lots of insects swarming around in an incredibly small area. All of them are make a living—because many of them don't compete for the same food or homestead. Your prospecting territory is like that—there are many non-competing organizations

chasing your customers and prospects for business. Seek them out and build relationships with them—you pass them leads, and they pass you leads. Simple, but effective.

DO Take No for an Answer

Forget all that sales twaddle about the challenge to the salesperson of a No! The real challenge is to resist trying to turn every No! around, recognizing when no really means No! If in doubt, qualify out. Quickly. If a prospect hasn't a compelling reason to buy from you, find one who does. Selling time, energy and resources are much too valuable, and there are always lots more prospects worthy of your efforts.

Don't Worry about Failing

Prospecting is a numbers game. However successful your campaign, you'll have mis-hits. Learn from them. Think of Thomas Edison when his inventions repeatedly failed to perform as he expected: *"I didn't fail a thousand times, I learned a thousand ways it wouldn't work."*

There's gold in them thar hills! Go get it.

> *"Dig where the gold is
> ...unless you just need
> some exercise."*
>
> JOHN M. CAPOZZI
> "WHY CLIMB THE CORPORATE
> LADDER WHEN YOU CAN
> TAKE THE ELEVATOR?"

Strategy 28

Decoys

Decoys

Is It the "Real Deal?"

Time is money, and the most annoying waste of money for a busy salesperson is in the pursuit of business that you were never going to win in the first place. As salespeople, we are continually faced with the problem of decoy opportunities— apparent opportunities that are fabricated for a variety of reasons. The sad truth is that you will occasionally receive a Request For Proposal (RFP) from customers or consultants, requesting that you bid to supply products or services which they have no intention of purchasing. The good news is that you don't have to be a victim—not if you take the time to review every opportunity that comes your way to ensure that it is not a decoy.

Why are Decoys Used?

Decoy RFPs are released for a great variety of reasons, the most common being:

- Research/Free Consultation/Information

  Some people issue RFPs to develop a view of the current state of developments in a given industry. Experience suggests that many consultants find the proposal process a very useful way to conduct basic research on behalf of their customers—research for which *they* get paid. However, you must be careful. Most RFPs are for real. You might feel more comfortable moving forward with an RFP if you know the consultant who has issued it and you consider him or her trustworthy, or it's clear someone has done a lot of work to prepare a convincing RFP, or if you are invited to meet the customer personally. But if you have any reservations, qualify carefully and don't be afraid to walk away—to spend your time on opportunities of which you are more certain. Qualify out early—on the simple basis that you will likely get a better return on your time pursuing other opportunities.

> Sometimes proposals are requested for reasons other than a desire to purchase—don't be a decoy victim.

- To Prepare a More Comprehensive RFP

A vague RFP, one in which there has been little time invested, from a substantial customer, for an obviously genuine requirement can often signal that the customer is looking to produce a more comprehensive RFP from a combination of all of the best aspects of any proposals submitted (it can also signal the opportunity of your life—so don't be too cynical). If you suspect that this is the case, you must decide whether or not the customer is worth the effort—you must weigh up whether you are prepared to give away your best ideas against the obvious benefits to having some input into the final RFP document.

- To Build a Specification for an In-house Project

  This is perhaps the most cynical use of the proposal process and it is not at all uncommon. The customer  prepares a comprehensive RFP document and solicits a number of very detailed responses and follow-up presentations. Very often, the decision to proceed is then put "on hold" during the evaluation process.

  All we can say on this one is that the type of organization that pursues this sort of policy very often fits the "repeat offenders" category. So, "Once bitten, twice shy."

How Do You Spot a Decoy?

There is no definitive way to spot a decoy RFP, but they generally have one or more of the following characteristics:

- The Bluebird

  Every so often, every salesperson is lucky enough to get a "Bluebird"—a deal which comes "out of the blue," never having appeared on any account plan or revenue projections, only to position itself to become the year's big earner. A decoy RFP is almost always a Bluebird. Watch out for them.

- Non-Customer

  Decoy RFPs will very often come from an organization that is not currently a customer—very often, a prospect which you have been trying to break into for some time.

- Size

  In order to cause an instant brain shutdown, to disable your normally very sharp qualification faculties, the decoy prospect will very often be large and the opportunity substantial. Think—"Why are they suddenly contacting me?"

- Short Timescale

  This is a high-value, strategic acquisition, yet the decision will be made on what seems to be an almost impossibly short timescale and your response is required on an unreasonably short timescale.

- Little on Paper

  A decoy RFP will often betray itself by the lack of effort invested in its preparation. The RFP will very often be high level, giving little detail on the supposed requirement.

- Detail

  Despite its own non-detailed nature, the decoy RFP will usually require a great amount of detail on your products, services and costs.

> *Large-scale deals that suddenly pop up on your radar, with short response timescales and little information are often decoys. Seller beware!*

- Limited Contact within the Prospect

  A tell-tale sign of a decoy RFP is the level of contact you are afforded within the prospect organization. If the requirement is so substantial, the value so large, and the timescale so tight, how come there are so few of the prospect's senior managers involved in the acquisition?

Don't Be a Decoy Victim

Unless you see benefit to proceeding with a proposal to meet an opportunity you feel is a decoy (building your profile within a strategic account, for example), then, in general, we suggest that you run away. Save your energies for those opportunities you are satisfied you have a real chance to convert into revenue.

Whatever you do, when you find yourself in pursuit of an opportunity that is, in fact, a decoy, be sure that it's for your reasons, that you have made the conscious decision to follow this course—that no one else is pulling the strings.

Strategy 29

Objection!

Objection!

What to Say
When They Say, "No!"

When you start out in selling, you are enthusiastic about your product, the future, and how wonderful everything is going to be...and then your prospects mess everything up by not buying from you. At least that's my story.

A Personal Story from Jim Sirbasku

In my sales training, I was told how to handle some of the more common objections, but it seemed as if I was calling on some of the most creative people in the world who handed me objections to which I had no idea how I should respond. I told my Sales Manager about the objections I was getting and asked him how to respond. He suggested that whenever I got an objection I couldn't handle on the spot, I should write it down. Later, I could think about the objection and write down one or more appropriate responses.

Over the next few weeks, I accumulated about 20 objections to which I had memorized some really dynamite responses. The next time I got an objection, I tested a new response. If it worked, I kept using it. If it didn't, I revised it and tried out the new version at my next opportunity. I got so good at objections, I looked forward to getting them because I knew exactly how to handle them.

After responding to an objection, I always asked a qualifying question such as, "Does that clear up the question in your mind?" If I got an affirmative response, I could continue toward the close, but if my prospect did not feel my dynamite response was adequate, I would ask another question: "What did I leave out?" That would usually get the prospect to tell me more about their objection and I would say, "Oh, I'm sorry. I meant to cover that." And then I'd respond and move on.

I have to say this method is almost perfect—I say almost because there are times when a prospect cannot, or will not, verbalize their real objection. When you use an effective method for dealing with objections and still don't close the sale, you can be pretty sure the prospect had a hidden objection they would not reveal to you. Just remember, you can't win 'em all, but then neither do the world champions.

In most businesses today, suppliers are selected on the basis of a proposal where purchasers outline their requirements and invite prospective suppliers to "bid" for their business. A winning proposal is based on a basic six-part model:

- Executive Summary
- Your Requirement
- Our Solution to Your Requirement
- Benefits of our Proposed Solution
- Costs
- Appendices.

There is a lot of edge to be gained by personally presenting the content of your proposal to a prospect. After all, few prospects will read every word of a proposal, and those they miss may well be the ones that set you apart from your competitors. A face-to-face presentation is an ideal opportunity to drive home the particularly positive points of your proposal.

Be Sure to Expect Objections

Once your customer has agreed to let you present a summary of your proposal, you need to begin preparing for objections. An objection can be your prospective customer's way of indicating that he or she is seriously interested in what you have to say, but needs more information about certain points in order to accept your arguments. Objections can also indicate that the prospect is totally disinterested in what you have to say, and is simply looking for a way to say No.

> An objection can be your prospective customer's way of saying, "I need more information."

When you are preparing, reviewing or rehearsing your presentation, take note of any point to which your customer could possibly raise an objection. Be sure that you have included all possible objections. Don't rely solely on your own judgment—ask other members of your team to identify points on which the customer might base objections.

When you have a comprehensive list of likely objections, develop positive responses to each one. If any of the objections are technical in nature, be sure to assimilate sufficient knowledge to be able to handle the objection yourself, or plan to invite one of your more technical colleagues to address the objection.

Handling Objections

If you have prepared adequately, you will be ready to address the majority of the objections raised. So, when they are raised, how do you handle them? Follow this five-step approach:

Step 1. Do and Say Nothing (for a moment)
Let them see you listen intently to the objection, nodding your head in understanding, and then think for a moment, considering the objection—saying nothing. There are two values to this momentary silence. In the first instance, it indicates that you are truly thinking about the objection; your response is not just a glib, rehearsed response. Secondly, this momentary silence will very often prompt the questioner, or another audience member, to expand upon their objection, even to the extent of indicating what they think your response should be.

> *Take a few moments in silence after you've heard the objection— more information often emerges to fill the gap.*

Step 2. Confirm Your Understanding of the Objection

To further drive home the impression that you are truly considering the objection, and that your understanding of the objection is correct, paraphrase the objection and present it back to the customer. Preface the paraphrased objection with "*Am I correct that your concern is...?*" or "*If I understand you correctly, you are concerned that....*" Never address an objection until you have qualified it as valid.

Step 3. Respond to the Objection Confidently and Authoritatively

Deliver your prepared response in a confident and authoritative tone. If the objection is one you had not anticipated, offer an immediate reasonable response, or offer to research the objection and return later with a response.

Step 4. Confirm that Your Response Satisfactorily Addressed the Objection

"*Does this answer your concern on...?*" If not, then return to Step 2 and re-state the objection, or a new definition of the

particular aspect of the objection that you have failed to address.

Step 5. Return to Where You Were in Your Presentation
One of the most important aspects of having prepared for objections is your ability to handle them, and still be able to return to the point to which your presentation had progressed before the interruption.

What if You Can't Agree?

If you do feel that you have addressed the objection, but the customer does not concur, avoid arguing the point—you can't win. Offer to research the objection further, and pointedly note the objection. Put as positive a face as you can on your response and move on.

What if You Have No Good Response?

If the customer introduces an objection for which you have no good response, try to present an equally positive aspect of your proposed solution to offset the negative impact of the objection. For example, *"Yes, MyCorp's solution is 20 percent more expensive than our next nearest competitor, but independent research has shown that the life of our product is 40 per cent longer than the nearest in the marketplace, and we are acknowledged as the market leader in ongoing support."*

Key Points in Objection Handling

- View every objection positively—they are all opportunities to drive home the more positive benefits of your proposal.

- Be very careful not to be seen to be defensive in responding to objections.

- Be enthusiastic about your company, and its products and services—regardless of what objections are raised. Don't accept negative comments about you, your company, or your products or services, without some positive counteractive response.

- Don't lie or exaggerate. If you don't have a ready answer, say so—committing to return with a response at a later date.

- The customer is always right—even when they're wrong. Don't argue with your audience.

The key to getting past objections is simple: don't ever give up. Stay in the game till the end.

Strategy 30

World-Class
Salespeople

World-Class
Salespeople

Spotting the 20% who Sell the 80%

Who would have predicted that Vilfredo Pareto's famous 80–20 rule, formulated more than 100 years ago, would still apply to sales organizations today?

Research consistently demonstrates that more than half of those in professional sales lack the basic attributes required for success in this difficult profession—attributes that *World-Class Salespeople* possess as natural gifts or develop through training or single-minded focus. Of the remaining half, half of these have the potential for success in some form of sales, but are currently selling the wrong product or service. That leaves about 25 percent to sell about 80 percent of the world's products and services.

> ### 25% of all salespeople sell 80% of all products sold. Scary!

Enlightening, isn't it?

That's why it's important for you to have a keen understanding of the attributes of *World-Class Salespeople*. If you can recognize them, you can hire more of them! You can also tell when salespeople on your team need training and support, and you'll have a good idea of what they need.

Measure your salespeople by this list of the ten attributes shared by *World-Class Salespeople*:

1. Irrepressibly Positive Attitude

All of their glasses are half-full and every cloud they encounter has a silver lining. Knock them down nine times and they stand up the tenth. Without this iron optimism, a life in sales is a stressful and daunting existence. *Do your sales heroes live in a partly cloudy or partly sunny world?*

2. Understand that Sales is a Numbers Game

They don't lose their cool when a call goes badly, a deal goes south, or a first contact ends in refusal—they simply focus more carefully on the next call. They know their hit rate from past experience—they know how often they'll have to take No! on the chin to get to one Yes! *Do your salespeople know the value of their calls?*

3. Live to Prospect

The World-Class Salespeople are prospecting all of the time—especially when things are going well. They know that sales success is directly dependent upon continually filling their pipelines with well-qualified prospects. Prospecting is their obsession—they never stop. *Is prospecting 24/7/365 in your organization?*

4. Totally Sales-Driven

These people live for the chase that results in a closed deal; they are internally motivated to go to whatever lengths they must to win the business. They seem to have unceasing energy—once they decide to act, nothing slows or stops them until they have succeeded.

Are your salespeople in top gear?

5. Competitive

They don't like second, and they are not good losers. Sure, they know they must affect a "good-loser" performance from time to time—for social reasons. But deep down, they need to win, and losses just stiffen their resolve. They can't be kept in second place for long.

Is your team too good at losing?

6. Obsessed with the "Next Step"

Everything they do is about getting to the "next step"—about getting the next level of commitment to bring the customer ever closer to the level of trust and confidence needed for a Yes! *World-Class Salespeople* think solely in terms of specifics like where, when, how, and how much. Concepts like sometime, in the future, later, whenever are simply not in their vocabularies. The most successful salespeople at Profiles know that their success is inevitable, but they still drive to "accelerate the inevitable."

> World-Class Salespeople are obsessed with the next step.

Are your salespeople driving their case forward at least one step with every customer or prospect contact?

7. Know that They and Their Products are World Class

Quiet confidence oozes out of top salespeople, and unbridled enthusiasm for their company, their products and services gushes from them at every meeting. No one is left untouched by the passion they pull upon when they talk about themselves, their companies, or their products and services. They evangelize.

Have your people been to the top of the mountain?

8. Qualify Hard before Investing Time and Energy

Time is too precious to waste on people who don't need what they provide. They understand their products and services inside out, understand the needs they address, understand why their offerings are so much better than those of their competitors, and know enough about their prospective customers to find themselves rarely in front of someone who is not a genuine prospective customer.

Do your salespeople look before they leap?

9. Expect to Hear No!

Once they know they are in front of the right people, these champions are confident that they have considered every possible No! situation that might arise, and they understand how to address these objections in a way to build the confidence and trust of their prospective customers.

Are your front people always ready to handle key objections?

10. Sell through Customer Knowledge

Ask customers of *World-Class Salespeople* what sets them apart and they'll tell you, "They understand us." These people never stop trying to find out more information about the customer and their needs—they know that the only way they can deliver sales is through partnership and problem-solving.

How much do your salespeople know about their customers and prospects?

When you hire salespeople, you must look for these attributes. While this sounds simple, how do you objectively measure these attributes?

Effectively Spot the 20%

That's a challenge we faced in building our 800-strong worldwide sales force at Profiles—and we met it head on with the development of the Profiles Sales Indicator (PSI). The PSI analyzes your existing salespeople to produce a profile of what it takes to be a successful salesperson in your organization. Using your prospective salesperson's responses to a 15–20-minute online survey, the PSI objectively analyzes the person for these attributes:

- Competitiveness
- Self-reliance
- Persistence
- Energy
- Sales Drive.

By comparing these results with the profile of your most successful salespeople, PSI can predict on-the-job performance in these critical sales disciplines:

222

- Prospecting

- Closing Sales

- Call Reluctance

- Self-starting

- Teamwork

- Building and Maintaining Relationships

- Compensation Preference.

All seven disciplines are essential to the success of the top-performing 20 percent of salespeople responsible for 80 percent of all sales.

The PSI's clear, readable reports can be used for selecting salespeople, as well as for effective management and training of existing salespeople to help them reach the performance levels of your top performers. PSI worked so well for Profiles that we're certain it will work well for your organization, too. You can read more about it on the web at: www.profilesinternational.com

Take action today to move all of your team into the 20 percent zone, and watch your sales soar.

"If winning isn't everything, why do they keep score?"
VINCE LOMBARDI
(1913–1970)

Strategy 31

The Sky is Not Falling

The Sky is Not Falling

Good Tactics for Bad Times

September 11, 2001 will live in the minds of people forever. Three thousand lives were lost and our psyche was struck that day. For a period of time, Americans were crippled with fear. The attacks caused people to be cautious and hesitant. The atmosphere debilitated our economy into stagnation. The momentum we had worked so hard to create in our business had come to a standstill. Where do we go from here?

We met with our staff to explore our options. The attacks of 9/11 had a lesser impact outside of the United States so we focused on further expanding our business internationally. We composed a list of 23 countries where economic and political conditions appeared to be conducive to the products and services our company markets. Through diligent research, we were able to identify and contact many excellent prospects. We interviewed and exchanged information with many superb prospects. Naturally, we assessed each of our candidates to help measure their suitability for success in our business. Finally, we invited all of our top candidates to Waco to met us personally and tour our facilities. As a result of these efforts, 20 of the original 23 countries targeted for expansion entered into business with Profiles International, Inc.

The message of this strategy is clear. Maintain your optimism regardless of the situation. It may seem like the sky is falling, but look for the opportunities you may be overlooking!

Here are ten tactics for coping in tough times—all of which your sales organization can quickly put into action. Some of these actions are specifically aimed at the sales-management level; others at every salesperson in the organization. To maximize your chances of success, you need to implement every one of them to balance the negative effects that weakened consumer confidence can have on your sales volume in tighter times.

1. Cross- and Up-Sell in Existing Active Accounts

Active purchasers/users of your products and services who are buying from you currently may have a need for something else that you do—and you don't yet know (and neither do they, likely as not). Get out and find out. Look at ways of up-selling and cross-selling into all of these accounts. How could they blend one service/product they currently use with another they've never used? What would be the benefit to them of doing so? What financial/other incentive can you give them to do so? Think about it, and then formulate as many cross- and up-sell strategies as you can for everything that you currently provide. Look at packaging sets of goods and services to have an impact, so that you add value and revenue to every single sale you make. With a little imagination, you'll find you can increase the value of every sale, and create brand-new sales, with little additional effort. It doesn't have to result in a doubling of the value of every sale you make, or in doubling the value of every existing account. Even modest margin increases will add up substantially over time. Look at how McDonald's and Burger

King approach every one of their admittedly individually modest sales—*"Would you like fries with that?"* or *"Would you like a pie with that?"* Do it now—talk to all customers currently buying from you and seek to up the value of every sale into every one of those accounts, one way or another. Go large!

2. Awaken Hibernating Accounts

Review the records of everyone you've ever done business with—you'll find there are some on that list who, for whatever reason, have had no contact from you or your sales force for some time. Good times are like that—we all tend to chase the "low-hanging fruit"—the opportunities that walk up to us and say, "Take me!" There will be some customers who have had excellent experience with you, but who haven't done anything with you recently because you simply didn't ask. Get out and see everyone. Things have changed since you saw them last—for one thing, you're much hungrier and, if you've actioned the first point above, you now have so many "packaged" offerings that you must have something to interest them.

A key point when you undertake these first two steps is to avoid the temptation to "come clean" and confess that things are tight. Do that and you put your most valuable assets in a situation where they may feel pressured to do something for you—particularly if traditionally you have had good personal relationships with the account contacts. Also, the thought that you might be under any real pressure can grow into the concern that you may not be around to service or implement any project or product that they might buy from you. Be upbeat and treat this as an account-development meeting—seeking more ways in which you can help these valuable customers to meet their objectives, thereby helping you to meet yours.

3. Revisit All Recent Leads

In good times, there is always some easy money to be made, and, therefore, prospects who express an interest in what we do and then either don't place an order or don't return our calls, and they fall by the wayside. Review all of your recent leads. Filter out those that came to nothing—but where, for whatever reason, you never got to a No! or to a formal decision on your part to qualify out. If these folks contacted you looking for information, or attended a seminar, or requested a brochure, then at some point they had a qualified interest. Chase down these leads once and for all. You'll find that some never got around to making their purchase because they were too busy and there was no salesperson driving their decision-making process. Be that salesperson.

4. Seek Referrals

This is classic, basic sales advice, but it is never more important than when times are tough. In every encounter with active customers or hibernating accounts, get into the habit of asking for referrals. During the good times, the basics get left behind.

229

Look to existing accounts for referrals to other contacts within the account, or for referrals to their suppliers and peer organizations. Speak with everyone you know in business and ask them to think of anyone to whom you should be speaking. It will get results. Simple, but effective.

5: Cast your Net Wider

When things are good, the advice is simple: refine your target audience. Know your customer base and market to it to the exclusion of all others. It also means being fussy—going only for the high-ticket, high-margin deals you deserve. When the going gets tough, go for some of those smaller projects you would have sniffed at in better times. Be prepared to come down from the mountain.

Take that horrified look off your face—we're not suggesting you compromise your values or your standard of service, simply that you recognize the reality that tighter times demand a more flexible approach to deciding upon who merits your attention. Nor are we suggesting you throw all discretion out the window, and market to all comers. There's no need for such drastic action—you'll find that lowering your sights even a little will substantially broaden the target base with which you have to work.

> Tough times demand flexibility—be prepared to come down from the mountain to consider business you might previously have ignored.

Be careful, however. What you sell to one class of prospects may not appeal to another, perhaps smaller, purchaser. Look carefully at your offerings, and at the new additions to your target base, and repackage what you do to appeal specifically to them. Is there a way to "modularize" what you do, breaking it down into smaller individually priced elements that smaller customers can use on an as-needed basis? Can you provide financial payment terms that make it easier for the customer with shallower pockets to work with you? What can you do to broaden your appeal?

Recognize that you may have to create a brand-new range of product/service offerings and marketing approaches to hit your now wider target base.

6. DON'T Reduce (or Increase) Costs

...but DO increase value. The moment you start the "bargain basement" approach, your existing customers will imagine that they smell "blood in the water" and this may shake their confidence—driving them further away than ever from doing business with you. No prospect or customer ever ran away from more "bang for his or her buck," however. Look at how you can deliver more—better service, higher quality, better payment terms, whatever—for the same money. Do this by looking at what your targets value and what your competitors deliver. You'll find that you can very often up your value proposition by 100 percent and still elevate your true cost of sale by only a fraction of that percentage. And—need we say it?—don't even consider pumping up your prices in tough times.

7. Invest More Time and Money

…in marketing and promotion. You've heard it all before: sales is a numbers game. These numbers—particularly the key ratio—are completely different when things tighten. If you were working a 100–10–1 model previously (100 suspects producing 10 prospects, which in turn produced 1 sale), then you know you're going to have to ramp the input to this funnel to a much higher level to compensate for the slowdown. Do you have to double it? Triple it? Whatever the multiplier, you'll find you need to have your prospecting machine running continually, in parallel with all other activities, seven days a week. Look at what you can realistically aim to sell to your target base and set about designing as many ongoing prospecting activities as possible. Ramp up your public relations, run value-added seminars and road shows, engage in coordinated mail and fax broadcasts—do whatever you have to do to get your message, and ultimately your sales team, in front of as many prospective customers as possible. If you haven't already done so, consider dedicating some of your team to prospecting alone. Now is not the time to stint on the promotional budget—now more than ever you have to invest in chasing prospects out into the open.

8. Build Lifetime Customers

In general, the easiest and most profitable business to win has always been that won from existing satisfied customers. Delivering excellent customer service is absolutely essential when there's less business to go around. If you are a direct part of the sales organization or effort in your company, you are one of those with ultimate responsibility for development of profitable customer relationships, and with customer retention. No longer can you pass the buck for implementation or delivery to someone else in the organization—to ensure your future sales, you must take complete ownership and responsibility for the success (as perceived by your customer) of all of your sales. This means taking a perhaps unprecedented interest in the successful and quality implementation or delivery of every project, product or service you deliver to your customers. It means ensuring that everyone involved in delivering what you sell understands that you expect them to "go the extra mile" to satisfy your customers spectacularly. Ensure that all of your sales result in delivering the success and benefit the customer set out to achieve—that way, you start making headway on tomorrow's sales today.

9. Ask the Troops What They Think

Before you charge into implementing these suggestions, see if your team has any more to add to the action plan. Call for input from every department in your company on what its people think you could do to up revenues and drive sales. Don't confine this to your sales and marketing people—frequently your technical and administration people have a keener awareness of what your customers would really like, or would be willing to pay extra for. Besides drumming up new ideas, this process will make everyone feel an important part of the organization's positive drive for increased success—people will much more effectively implement actions they feel they helped to formulate than ones they feel have been imposed upon them.

233

10. Keep Your Chin Up

Hey! We're not Pollyannas, we're not *positive-thinking-in-the-face-of-ridiculous-odds* nut-balls, but we can assure you that unless you stay optimistic, you're dead. Don't feel that you or your business is unique in its suffering, and that all is lost—it's that kind of thinking that fuels dips in consumer confidence. Whatever you're facing, you'll find that others have come through worse, and that things always get better—and this happens all the faster for those who keep their heads and remain focused and optimistic. Too many people fold up their tents and head for home at the first sign of bad weather. Don't be one of them. Businesses can survive, and even thrive, if their owners and managers remain calm and do what needs to be done to cope with more challenging times. Decide what you need to do to ride the storm out, and then focus all of your energies upon doing it.

The sky is never really falling, unless we collectively wish it down upon ourselves.

Strategy 32

The New Art of
Hiring Smart

The New Art of Hiring Smart

Good People Grow Business

It's the best of times and the worst of times, too—if people problems are coming between you and the commercial success that you see your peers enjoying. If you're either experiencing excessive staff turnover or finding that the people you're hiring simply "don't fit in," use the following six steps, The New Art of Hiring Smart, to ensure that you get more of the people you need.

1. Determine the True Cost of Turnover

The Saratoga Institute (www.saratogainstitute.com) publishes a simple formula for calculating turnover cost. Take the annual salary for any job where you have excessive turnover, add a typical 30 percent for benefits, and calculate 25 percent of the total. That's the absolute minimum it costs you every time that position turns over—if you provide any other benefits, or incur any other costs, it's actually much more. Multiply this figure by the number of times the position turns over. Do this for every job where you have turnover. Scary, huh? Add other costs, like share of overhead, recruitment costs (agency fees, advertising, travel, etc.), training costs, lost production/opportunity cost while the position is empty, and morale costs. Now that we have your attention, let's do something about the problem.

2. Identify Hiring Problems and Mistakes

Identify any part of your organization that's having people problems and find out what's causing them by:

- Asking your department and human resource managers why, in their opinion, these departments have turnover, why people quit, get fired, or become problematic.

- Conducting exit interviews—ask each person who leaves the company what could you have done to help them succeed and to prevent them from leaving. Don't be fooled by "pay more money."

- Asking your top people what they like about their jobs and how you can make their jobs better—try to replicate whatever they like throughout the organization.

- Looking at the people doing the hiring, and asking them (or asking yourself): Do they need training? Do they have a system that works? Do they take hiring new people seriously?

3. Recruit People Who Fit Your Jobs

- *First, You Must Understand the Job and Develop a Competency-Based Job Description*
  It is critical that you document the competencies required by all of your jobs from a technical, educational, experience, and industrial know-how basis—otherwise, how can you know what you're looking for?

- *Match People to Jobs*
  Harvard Business Review conducted a huge study—360,000 people, in 14 industries during a 20-year period—

in an attempt to identify what made for job success. The study discovered that people are successful only when they are matched to their jobs. They must have the right level of learning abilities; have a motivational interest in the work; and their behavioral make-up or personality must equip them to do the job well.

You cannot get the information necessary to match people to jobs from candidates' résumés, or from conventional interviews. The only way you can uncover this information is by formal assessment of candidates using assessments designed specially for the task. *The Profile* was designed specifically for this task—you can find more information about it at:

www.profilesinternational.com/products/profileXT.asp

4. Prospect Innovatively for Candidates

Consider additional sources you may not be using, such as:

- *Employee Bonus for Referrals of Candidates You Employ*
- *Physically or Mentally Disadvantaged*

- *Senior Citizens*

  The retired community is a rich source of motivated candidates for many empty positions.

- *Companies that have Announced Cutbacks*

  Contact the personnel and department managers in organizations announcing cutbacks and describe the candidate you are seeking.

- *Set Up Educational Relationships*

  Find the universities, colleges, or schools that support your industry through their curricula, and develop relationships with them.

5. Prepare for and Conduct a Winning Interview

Preparing for an interview is just as important as the interview itself.

- *Review the Job Description*

  In advance of the interview, clarify in your mind the job requirements, and the kind of competencies you expect to find in the person who will fill the job.

- *Develop Lead Questions*

  Lead questions are based on the job description— designed to bring out answers that will lead to follow-up questions.

The interview itself has three parts:

- *The Open*

  No candidate likes doing interviews—they are viewed simply as a necessary evil. The Open has two objectives:

first, to put the applicant at ease and build rapport. The better the rapport you create, the better the information you receive. Second, you want to set the agenda and timetable. Explain the sequence for the interview and approximately how long you will be together.

Your overall objectives for the Open are to create excitement about the job and put your candidate at ease.

● *The Body*

Ask your lead questions here. When doing so, think:

◆ *Can this person do the job?*

Have they the necessary qualifications, experience, and competencies that you know are necessary for success in the position? Do their learning abilities match those demanded by the job?

◆ *Will this person do the job?*

If you're satisfied that the candidate has the qualities to do the job successfully, your next task is to ensure that he or she is motivated to be successful in the position. Is the nature of the work sufficiently motivating for them to ensure success? This can usually be determined only through assessment of the candidate's motivational interests, using assessments like *The Profile* (mentioned above). The purpose of the interview in this regard is then to probe any areas of concern uncovered by the assessment process.

◆ *Will this person fit our corporate culture?*

Being capable and motivated to do the job well is sufficient only if you are confident that the candidate will also be a good fit to your company. Again, the extent of this match is best determined using a pre-interview assessment like *The Profile*, with the interview providing an opportunity to probe any areas where the candidate seems to be a poor match to the position. Listen carefully and take notes. Later, review your notes carefully and form your opinions.

- *The Close*

  The Close is no less important than the two previous stages of the interview, allowing for both sides to summarize and agree next steps.

  In a book we highly recommend—*Hire with Your Head* by Lou Adler—there's a suggested closing statement that can be used with all candidates, especially those who will make the next cut:

  > Hire with Your Head, *by Lou Adler, is an excellent source of information.*

  > *"Although we're seeing other fine candidates, I personally think that you have a very fine background. We'll get back to you in a few days, but what are your thoughts about this new position?"*

  This close creates a sense of competition and job attractiveness; expresses sincere interest in the candidate; and allows the interviewer to gauge how much interest the candidate has in the position.

6. Continually Refine Your Practices

Books like Lou Adler's *Hire with Your Head*, and seminars and workshops on best-practice hiring, run by organizations like Profiles, will help you continually to refine your skills in this area. Your local Profiles office can let you know what events are scheduled in your area (find your local representative by sending an e-mail to:

Profiles@ProfilesInternational.com).

People are your most important asset—shouldn't you invest at least as much effort in attracting, recruiting and retaining them as you invest in winning and retaining customers?

Strategy 33

What Goes Around

What Goes Around

See Your Managers' Strengths
from Every Angle

A senior manager announces his decision to move to a competitor and the senior management team convenes a crisis-management meeting to figure how the organization will survive. Meanwhile, for the rest of the team, it's party time! The champagne is flowing, everyone's wearing funny hats, blowing noisemakers, and toasting their good fortune. The topic *du jour* is *"With that clown gone, maybe now we can get on with business."*

What happened? How can someone so valued by senior management work so badly with the troops on the ground? The reality is most senior managers have no awareness of how they or their fellow managers are perceived throughout their organizations—even at a time when so much is spoken about achievement of corporate goals through team-based efforts. It's no wonder that more than 30 percent of all people changing jobs are doing so to get away from their bosses. They're not leaving their jobs—they're leaving their managers!

This sort of disaster can happen only in an environment where the performance of management is appraised using traditional "boss-down" appraisals, with performance of managers assessed only by their direct bosses. This traditional approach means that the views of those who most directly experience the effectiveness (or otherwise) of a

244

manager's performance—peers and direct reports—are never tapped. If your success depends to any extent upon your team, that's just not acceptable any more.

Multi-Rater Feedback

Modern business has rendered the traditional "boss-down" appraisal extinct, and a more appropriate approach to assessing management competencies and performance has emerged. That new approach is *Multi-Rater Feedback*, and *Profiles Checkpoint* is an excellent example of this new model.

CHECKPOINT MULTI-RATER FEEDBACK

Every year, more than 250,000 managers worldwide use the *Profiles Checkpoint Multi-Rater Feedback System*—a system that provides managers and leaders with an opportunity to receive an evaluation of their job performance from the people around them—their Boss, their Peers (fellow managers), and their Direct Reports (the people whose work they supervise). From this feedback, managers can compare the opinions of others with their own perceptions, positively identify their strengths, and pinpoint the areas of their job performance that could be improved.

The *Profiles Checkpoint* process is concerned with a manager's job performance in eight universal leadership and management competencies, and 18 skill sets:

Communication
- Listens to others
- Processes information
- Communicates effectively

Leadership
- Instills trust
- Provides direction
- Delegates responsibility

Adaptability
- Adjusts to circumstances
- Thinks creatively

Relationships
- Builds personal relationships
- Facilitates team success

Task Management
- Works efficiently
- Works competently

Production
- Takes action
- Achieves results

Development of Others
- Cultivates individual talents
- Motivates successfully

Personal Development
- Displays commitment
- Seeks improvement

How Does it Work?

Each participant completes an evaluation—a process that takes about 15 minutes. Participants are guaranteed anonymity (except for the Boss) and urged to be honest and objective in their responses. Participants complete their feedback via the Internet, or on paper if desired, and results from all participants are compiled in a report that is returned to the manager.

Checkpoint reports have colorful graphs and useful charts, as well as narrative descriptions of the results, to help the manager to read, understand, and effectively use the data for self-development. The report has a special personal-growth section that coaches the manager and helps improve performance in development areas.

> *Modern business has rendered the traditional top-down appraisal extinct.*

The *Checkpoint* report also encourages managers to link directly into an online system called *Checkpoint SkillBuilder,* which takes them through the step-by-step process of developing a comprehensive and personalized development plan. You can read more about the Checkpoint system on the Web at: www.profilesinternational.com

Round and Round...

The upshot is a more detailed and objective assessment of a manager's strengths, and of any areas where additional development might be required. This assessment then forms the basis of a development plan agreed between managers and their bosses—whereas the managers are fully aware of the dynamics of their relationships with the

people around them, they are also effectively locked into the organization by the commitment of the organization to their ongoing skill development.

After a period of 6 or 12 months, the process is run again; the effectiveness of the development plan is assessed; and new development goals are set for the following period.

Multi-Rater Feedback vs. "Boss-Down" Appraisals

There are several reasons why managers at all levels are eagerly embracing this approach to performance appraisal.

Equitable

For the manager being appraised, *Multi-Rater* appraisals differ from boss-down appraisals in the same way that judge and jury courts differ from "hanging judge" courts. Managers benefit from a wide variety of feedback upon their actual job performance, and, to be deemed top-performing managers, are no longer solely dependent upon the extent to which they have developed a good rapport with their direct boss.

Proven Effectiveness

For the appraising boss, a positive change is more likely when an appraisal draws upon multiple sources trusted by the manager. *Multi-Rater* appraisals have been shown to be more effective than boss-down appraisals in driving a manager to make necessary behavioral changes or to improve management skills. If your boss says you need some improvement in some particular area, you may think, *"What would she know?"* or explain it away as a *"personality thing."* If, however, eleven different people of your choosing—people with whom you work closely and whose views you trust and value—send you the same message, you really have to listen.

> The cycle is key:
> Feedback...
> Review...
> Plan & Develop...
> Review...
> Feedback...
> and so on.

Team Motivation

Multi-Rater Feedback systems also have a positive team-building effect. Research has proven the motivating value of the exercise for those involved as reviewers. Your people are sent a clear message that their opinions are valued, and they can help effect positive change in the management where required. Traditional reviews have given way to this much more effective tool for management development, as Fortune 500 organizations are mandating their use.

Used regularly as an integral part of a strategic development plan, 360-degree appraisals can lead to more consistent management development, better alignment of corporate goals with personal-development objectives, more open communication, and better team balance.

Strategy 34

Day Before Vacation

Day Before Vacation

Prioritize and Commit for Success

In April 2002, Jim and I were honored when we were inducted into the Sales Hall of Fame in Oklahoma City. After the ceremony, we looked at the exhibits and a striking representation of the motivational guru Zig Ziglar (www.zigziglar.com), delivering a speech, inspired us to include the following strategy.

For decades, Zig has motivated and inspired millions of people to be better at whatever it is they do for a living. Zig's ideas about creating a sense of urgency are exemplified in his "Day Before Vacation" story. This technique can have a tremendous effect on your productivity, so use it!

Think about your last day at work before you went on your most recent vacation. Didn't you get as much done in that day as you'd normally get done in two, three, or even four days? (Be honest!) Look at what Zig says you did on the day before vacation.

On the night preceding the day before your vacation, you likely sat down with a piece of paper and listed all of the things that had to get finished the following day—your *gotta*s ("I gotta do this, and I gotta....") Then you committed that they'd all be done by the time you left the office the next day. Right?

On the morning of the day before your vacation, you arrived at the office on time—maybe even early. But you didn't head for the coffee machine—no, you got straight into the first *gotta* on your list. You likely also did things in a slightly different order  from usual—you took the least favored, most distasteful task on your list and got it out of the way quickly, instead of having it hanging overhead all day long (the way you normally would!) With that tough one out of the way, you were feeling pretty good, and so you tore into the next task on your list, and the next one after that. If anyone came to chat about last night's game, you politely but firmly informed them that you were just too busy—and got back to business.

As you completed each of your *gotta*s, you felt your energy rising, so that by halfway through the day you were buzzing with a sense of accomplishment that drove your enthusiasm level ever higher, raising your mood and painting a smile on your face. Your obviously energized and enthusiastic demeanor infected your colleagues—they started to ramp up the effort, to smile a little more, and they became similarly enthusiastic. The atmosphere in the office got a little extra spark, and this lifted you even further.

At the end of the day, you had all of your *gotta*s completed. You were as high as if you'd been on high-octane caffeine—even if you hadn't had a drop all day! You felt good.

Now, that's focus!

So, what did you do that day to get so focused? Let's have a look.

First, You Created a *Vision*

"By the time I leave tomorrow, I'll have cleared my desk and put my affairs in order so that I am free to be away for two weeks."

When your vision gets knocked offline by events around you, you are like a $10 billion guided missile without a target—you can fly around in circles looking pretty impressive, but eventually you're going to run out of fuel and crash and burn. If your vision has been hammered by recent economic changes, get working on a new one—now! Take time to figure out what you really want for yourself, your family and your business. Get it clear in your head and paint this target in front of you every day.

Second, You Formulated a Set of Goals

...that would deliver your vision—your *gottas*. Having a great vision is useless unless you formulate clear, achievable goals to ensure that your vision becomes reality. You must plot a course to take you from where you are now to your target, with checkpoints that let you know when you go off course.

Third, You Made a Commitment

"I absolutely must get these tasks completed by the time I leave the office tomorrow."

This is the most common stumbling block that people tend to hit, even if they are accustomed to planning by creating compelling visions and formulating achievable goals. They fail to commit. If you've ever made a New Year's resolution you failed to complete, you know what happens to plans without commitment. If there's no commitment, the fault is most likely with your vision—it simply isn't compelling enough; otherwise, the commitment naturally would follow. If you were fatally ill and had just one month to live, but could get a cure if you had $1 million more than your current total net worth, would you get the money? Of course you would—or you'd kill yourself trying even before the month was out! You know that your vision is right when it has the same sense of compelling urgency. A real commitment immediately gets you off the ground and in search of your target.

A real commitment gets you immediately off the ground in search of your target.

Before you spend one more day out of focus, stop and look carefully at your life. Be sure that your guidance mechanism has a clear target encoded into it, and that you've mapped a route to target that makes you want to take off right now! Get the Day-Before-Vacation feeling every day!

*"We must use
time as a tool,
not as a crutch."*
JOHN F. KENNEDY

Strategy 35

Killer Sales Campaigns

Killer Sales Campaigns

How is Your Sales Heart Beating?

Sales are the beating heart at the center of every successful organization, and successful sales campaigns keep the heart beating.

The success or failure or your campaign is decided long before you decide what initiatives you're going to pursue. It is decided when you set your goals for the campaign. Clear goals make successful campaigns. The following simple steps will help you to create killer sales campaigns every time.

> *The success or failure of a sales campaign is determined long before you decide precisely what initiatives you'll pursue.*

Before you get started, here's an important question to ask: "How will I know when my campaign has been successful?"

Decide precisely what objective the campaign must achieve, long before you launch the campaign. Typical objectives might revolve around selling a particular number of units, achieving a given revenue target, building a specific prospect pipeline, etc. Clearly define the objective of the campaign in terms like, "We'll know the campaign is successful when…"

- "...we have sold 200 units of X product."

- "...we have added 50 new customers to our customer base."

- "...we have achieved revenues of X, with a margin of Y."

You may have multiple objectives for a given campaign—be sure that they are all SMART—**S**pecific, **M**easurable, **A**chievable, **R**ealistic, and **T**imed.

Then ask yourself: "What do I have to do to achieve this goal?"

Say your campaign objective is to sell 200 units of a particular product." Now follow these six steps to determine what actions your campaign will need to include to ensure success.

1. Look at Your Typical Sale—How Many Units of Product Does it Entail?

Say your typical sale is 10 units to a customer. Divide this figure into your end target—this will tell you how many customers you need to achieve your target. In our example, to sell 200 units when a typical sale is 10 units will require 20 new customers.

2. Look at Your "Close Rate"

Your close rate is the percentage of qualified prospects that ultimately become customers. If you don't have accurate figures from your records, estimate your close rate on the basis of your experience. Always estimate conservatively. For example, in our business, seven years of research show that we achieve a 2-in-5 close rate (40 percent) with well-qualified prospects. If that's your close rate, then in our example you will need to present to 50 well-qualified prospects. By the way, well-qualified means that they need your product, can afford your product, and are prepared to meet with you to discuss what benefits it might bring to them.

3. Look at Your "Qualification Rate"

Look at how many initial contacts or "touches" with suspects (suspected prospects) you will need to have in order to provide 50 well-qualified prospects. In our business, we use mailings, broadcast faxes and seminars to reach suspects. We achieve a 1-in-10 "hit rate" in identifying prospects who potentially need the service that we provide, and are prepared to meet with us to discuss their requirements—these are our "well-qualified" prospects. Applying this information to the example means you're going to need to "touch" 500 suspects over the course of the campaign to achieve your campaign objective.

4. Convert this Information into an Overview of the Activity Your Campaign Should Be Driving

Assume you plan to spread this campaign over 10 months. You know that your campaign must generate:

- 500 suspect "touches" overall—an average of 50 per month, or approximately 13 per week;

- 50 prospect presentations overall—an average of 5 per month, or approximately 2 per week;

- 20 new customers overall—an average of 2 per month, or approximately 1 every 2 weeks.

5. Decide Which Initiatives Will Deliver the Results

Now you have an idea of what you'll have to do to achieve your objectives and sub-objectives. The challenge is to figure out what actions will deliver these results. Look at the sort of initiatives that might create the required number of touches, presentations and close opportunities. Typical approaches include:

- Mailings and fax broadcasts

- Seminars and in-store promotions

- Advertising and public relations

- Whatever else has worked for you or your competitors in the past.

This is where you spend whatever budget you have to invest in your campaign. Look at which initiatives will give you the "best bang for your buck" in terms of hitting the specific numbers of suspects and prospects that you know you need. If one or another of these initiatives has previously shown itself to be more successful, spread your budget accordingly.

6. Keep an Eye on Progress

Take the attitude that your campaign plan represents your best guess at what will be successful for you, and review its progress with the open-minded attitude that you'll change it should it not prove as successful as you had originally hoped. Review your progress regularly—weekly, if appropriate. Have you hit your "touch," prospect presentation, and close rates for this week? If not, why not? Do you need to make any course corrections? Do you need to double your efforts next week? Is the original campaign strategy still valid? If not, change course immediately. Review progress on a frequent basis and you'll assure your campaign success.

Killer sales campaigns are less about the actual initiatives you undertake, and more about knowing precisely what you're trying to achieve, having a clear means for measuring your progress towards achieving it, reviewing your progress on a regular basis, and having the guts to change direction midstream if progress demands it.

Take this sensible approach and the success is assured— all of your campaigns will be natural-born killers.

Strategy 36

Put Your Customers on the Map

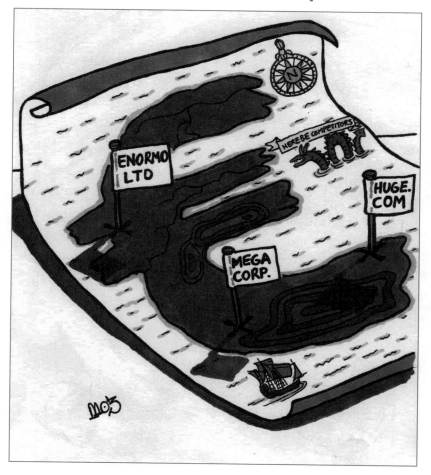

Put Your Customers on the Map

Chart a Course to Large-Account Success

You must put your major customers on the map, or someone else will.

Our world has changed. The emphasis on the acquisition of new customers at any cost is no more. Suddenly, there's the universal realization that existing customers are faster and easier to sell to; that business is much less expensive to win from existing customers than from strangers. The new order is 1-to-1 marketing and loyalty to ensure retention of those customers who will consistently generate good-margin business. The only way to retain valuable customers is by building solid, lasting and mutually beneficial relationships with them. But that's not easy.

> *The only way to retain valuable customers is to build solid, lasting and mutually beneficial relationships.*

Developing relationships takes time and effort, and is consequently extremely expensive. Limited resources mean that you have to be sure that the customers you choose to develop are worth the effort—that they will give you a good return over time. Trying to be all things to all customers just won't work—spread yourself too thin and you're setting yourself up for a fall. The investment is such that you simply can't afford to fail—you're almost betting the shop.

The key to success in your selected large accounts is understanding the power dynamics of the target organization: who makes the decisions, who assists, and who holds the power? This implies that the team selling to such key accounts has a solid handle on the structure of the decision-making group in the account, is clear on how each member of that group views the selling organization, and has a uniform plan to apply the resources at their disposal systematically to the effective development of relations with each member of the decision-making group.

To be effective, an account team must face a number of significant challenges.

1. Identify All Members of the Decision-making Group
   There's no point in selling hard to one or more members of the group if an unknown member can exercise a veto.

2. Rank Them in Order of Influence/Importance
   Knowing who makes the decisions, and who plays what role in the decision-making process is crucial.

3. Identify What Motivates Them
   Mass marketing insists that we all think the same, that we will all share a common view of the world. One-to-one marketing recognizes that everyone has

individual turn-ons, and that each individual must be sold to accordingly. There's no point offering the Chief Financial Officer the most comfortable truck on the market, or offering the driver the least expensive truck on the market—sell to their respective motivations.

4. Determine How They Feel About You and Your Company
If a key decision-maker has no time for you or your organization, work is needed. If, however, they think you're wonderful, then less effort may be required—freeing up resources to be used elsewhere.

5. Produce a Plan to Develop Each Contact Continually
Knowing their needs and views helps you to plan accordingly.

6. Communicate This Plan to Ensure a Consistent, Focused Team Effort
To help them succeed team-members need a relationship map (see example below) that will allow them to view the account from a different focus, using a common set of relationship-development objectives.

Mapping Your Accounts

Use this Relationship Map to make your work easier. Across the bottom of the map is a gauge of how the various contacts in the account feel about your organization and its offerings—*Negative* through *Indifferent* to *Positive*. Up the side of the map is a list of useful classifications for the range of players found in most decision-making groups:

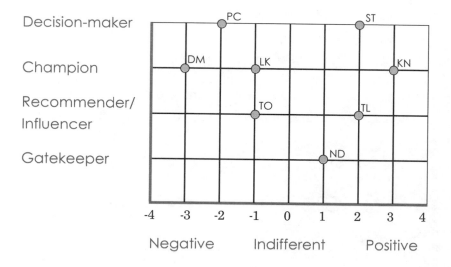

- A *Decision-maker* is the person who can give you a Yes. Anyone having the power of veto would also fall under this heading. There is often more than one individual who may exercise this power.

- A *Champion* is generally a *Decision-maker* or *Recommender/Influencer* who has chosen to drive a project or offering within their organization.

- *Recommenders/Influencers* are any other persons who have an input in the decision, but have no absolute Yes or No power. Examples might include end-users—the person who must ultimately use the PC or drive the purchased truck.

- The *Gatekeeper* defines who is allowed to play the game. Typically, this person is a purchasing manager or the head of the department who will be most affected by the planned purchase (for example, the IT Manager if the acquisition is a computer). It could also be a politically strong administration person like the CEO's assistant.

All members of the decision-making group can be placed on this map by assigning them a rank and a *Negative/Positive* rating. Once the team has agreed on each decision-maker's placement on the map (and it is imperative that mapping is on the basis of a team view), it becomes apparent to all where the selling organization stands, and what must occur to improve the standing. The team-members should strive to ensure that they have the entire decision group mapped, and that all are as far to the right on the map as possible. Again, resources may dictate that not all group-members can be developed equally, so decisions can be made on the relative investment required to improve the overall *Positive* index of the map.

> Put all key account contacts on your map and rate them Negative, Positive or Indifferent.

Mapped contacts are moved rightwards by development of a plan for each contact. This plan should:

- Recognize each contact's personal motivations.

- Include a number of specific "to-dos"—actions designed to improve the relationship with the contact. These actions should be practical, measurable, and should be assigned deadlines.

- Outline what information is required in order to improve the standing with the individual, and identify which team-member(s) is/are best placed to handle the task. The plan should also ensure that all of those having any day-to-day contact with the account understand what information is required—this should be to the front of the minds of sales and support people making calls on decision-makers.

> *Focus your efforts on those initiatives that drive key account contacts as far right on your map as possible.*

- Be reviewed by the team on a regular basis, with the map updated on the basis of team input—and progress measured by comparison with previous maps.

Map your major customers, and watch them put you, and your efforts, on the map.

> *"You can close more business in two months by becoming interested in other people than you can in two years by trying to get people interested in you."*
>
> DALE CARNEGIE

Strategy 37

Carrot, Stick
or What?

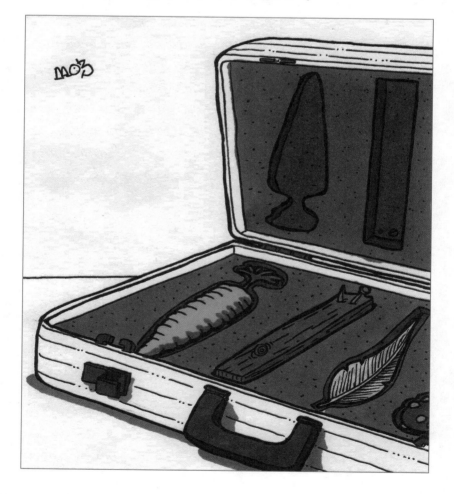

Carrot, Stick or What?

To Push or to Pull— That is the Question!

How would you like to have all of your team chomping at the bit to do what you need them to do to make your business successful? Everyone wants that elusive ingredient—motivation—in the people to whom they entrust the development of their businesses. Well, sorry to turn the lights to dim so quickly, but here's the bad news: YOU CANNOT MOTIVATE ANYONE TO DO ANYTHING—*people do what they do because they want to, not because you want them to. And they'll only want to do what you want them to do when the outcome of doing so appeals to them in some way. It is all in their hands, not yours.*

A Personal Story from Bud Haney

In the late 1960s, I began operating a franchise business, built a sales organization, and established a very successful operation in a short period of time. I did so well, the company made me a generous offer to become a sales executive in its home office. I joined a staff of experienced sales managers, so I was eager to prove myself as the new kid on the block. About a month after I joined the staff, the opportunity presented itself. The vice president of our division announced a contest, the grand prize being a TV set. Frankly, the TV set didn't excite me; I already had several of them at home. The opportunity to show my peers what I could do was my motivation.

I won the contest. I accomplished my goal by burning the midnight oil and motivating the members of my sales team to expand their efforts. I got them emotionally involved in the contest by asking them to do me a favor. I told them how important it was for me to gain the respect and acceptance of my peers and how much I would appreciate it if they would make an extra effort to be especially productive for 30 days. They came through for me, and everyone on the staff sat up and took notice of my arrival as a player on the scene.

Incidentally, the charitable organization that received the TV really appreciated it!

For practical business purposes, motivation is *getting people to do what you want them to do, because they want to do it.*

We are all motivated to action by two types of motivators—*intrinsic* and *extrinsic*. Extrinsic motivation happens when an outside factor causes us to take action—for example, "*Work an extra six hours and I'll pay you double time.*" Most management "motivation" is purely extrinsic, and amounts to little more than manipulation—enlisting promises, bribes and flattery to get things done.

> Motivation is getting people to do what you need them to do—because they want to.

273

The problem with extrinsic motivation is that it rarely has any useful long-term effect. Use extrinsic motivators to energize your team and you'll find yourself trapped in a cycle where those "motivators" must get bigger and better to repeat the same results. How long does the motivational effect of a salary increase last? Often only as long as it takes to see the post-tax figure! Traditional extrinsic approaches to motivation are all but useless aids to boosting long-term employee morale and productivity, or to stemming employee turnover.

How about intrinsic motivation? This happens when you take action because of internal reasons—for example, when you work an extra six hours because you feel that the project you're working on is so worthwhile you want to see it completed. Everything we do is ultimately determined by the values we hold. Values are what we truly care about— the qualities and standards we value and aspire to achieve. These values determine our attitudes and behaviors, and determine what will motivate us to action. When people take action because the likely outcome of that action appeals directly to what they value, you have true motivation—and time spent developing that is an investment with long-term returns. The most successful leaders and motivators are those who (wittingly or unwittingly) uncover their followers' intrinsic motivations, and take time to match these with the extrinsic motivators they have at their disposal.

Easy? Not at all. People are motivated by unmet needs and, unfortunately, these will vary from person to person according to their particular circumstances, values and beliefs, education, family background, personality, and work experience. The only way to figure out what is important to your people is to ask them, and then listen carefully. Ask often enough, and show your willingness to take action upon whatever you uncover, and your people will begin to let you know what is important to them—allowing you to figure out how to package those extrinsic "motivators" you have at your disposal in a manner that will meet their particular needs. This dialogue can be fostered with mechanisms as simple as frequent one-on-one discussions or well-considered surveys. There are no quick fixes, and this is not a one-time exercise; to be successful this has to become an integral part of the way you do business.

While working upon uncovering what your particular people need to be motivated, be aware that recent research has shown that what motivated people even as recently as 10 years ago is no longer necessarily relevant today. For example, modern employees view it as a right to have market-level remuneration in return for their efforts—so compensation is no longer a true motivator. In addition to a good salary and benefits package you must now also provide:

> *Everyone now routinely expects market-level remuneration—so money's no longer much of a motivator.*

- Development Opportunities—if you don't develop your people at the pace they desire, they'll find someone who can. People want to grow.

- Balance—new research shows that the modern worker's priorities are: leisure, family and work—in that order. Make number three the priority at the expense of one and two and you may strongly motivate them—*to move elsewhere.*

- Input to Decisions—modern employees feel they deserve input into any decisions that might affect them. Ignore this right at your peril.

- Communication with Management—modern employees are educated and confident and demand ongoing communication with their management.

- Worthwhile Goals—to hold their attention, people need the buzz of worthwhile short-term goals, and lots of feedback on their success (or failure) in achieving these goals.

- Interesting Work—much of the research on employee satisfaction over the past 5 years has emphasized the important role that interesting, challenging work plays in motivating people.

Take these three seemingly straightforward steps to build a highly motivated team:

1. Right Now: Honestly review the checklist above and if anything on it is not a feature of the way you interface with your team, figure out how you can make it so in the shortest time possible.

2. ASAP: Establish a program to ensure that you establish a frequently updated profile of what motivates each member of your team, and use this information to match the extrinsic motivators you have at your disposal to best meet their requirements.

3. Ongoing: Look carefully at the extrinsic motivators you have at your disposal and use your knowledge of your people's values and needs to match them to their intrinsic needs.

This will energize your team and assure your success. Now, is that a carrot, or what?

"*I have come to the conclusion that my subjective account of my motivation is largely mythical on almost all occasions. I don't know why I do things.*"

J.B.S. HALDANE

Strategy 38

The Final Hurdle

The Final Hurdle

Don't Fall at the Last Fence

Y ou're in the home stretch: your prospect has bought into what you're offering, and there's only one last hurdle—the final negotiation. Ask any seasoned campaigner, and they'll tell you that this is where all too many great deals suddenly die. What's the secret of sailing safely over the last hurdle?

The secret is that there is no secret—just a set of simple rules to observe, and some preparations to undertake. Final negotiations are no different from any other part of the sales cycle. Success depends largely upon careful planning. Understand how much (if any) you're prepared to concede, and be prepared to walk away if you can't reach agreement within these bounds. Know what you would like to achieve, and what you can reasonably expect, given limitations such as your customer's budget.

Consider your game plan—the order in which you will address the various elements in the upcoming negotiation— and plan a path through the negotiation to lead your prospect to accept your negotiation objectives. In order to be successful, you need to have walked through each and every play, anticipating objections and formulating responses that return you to your planned course and desired outcome.

In the words of a seasoned campaigner: "*If sales is courtship, then negotiation is foreplay—the slower it goes, the better.*" Generally, the only reason for maintaining the rapid pace of the sales cycle into the final negotiation is the concern that the deal might slip away if not closed now. Relax—if there weren't a genuine interest in doing business, you'd hardly be in a final negotiation, right? Slow it down.

> *Relax into negotiation— if they weren't interested, would you even be talking?*

Some purchasers like to introduce a little drama into a final negotiation by raising points not previously on the table. You can do a lot to address this problem before it happens. Be sure to:

- Know their requirements inside out. Understand how badly they need what you're offering.

- Know their budgets and timescales.

- Know the strengths and weaknesses of what you're offering, and how you stack up against your competition.

- Know who makes the final decision, and who else has any input.

The only way to get this information is to ask for it at every opportunity—up to, and including, the final negotiation itself. When you've asked, simply shut up and listen. Ambushes are not effective if you see them coming.

When the negotiation swings toward price, ask for confirmation that all other obstacles have been cleared. If you understand what is most important to your customer, and

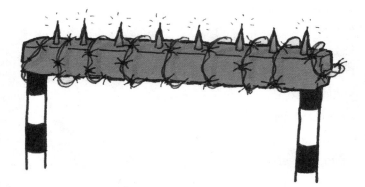

have effectively sold other aspects of your offering like delivery timescales, quality, solution, and so forth, you'll have a better feel for how much importance the customer places on price per se, and you'll better understand whether or not you have to move on price at all, and by how much.

When clearing all pre-price obstacles, remember that while you may have a perfect match to your customer's requirements, you cannot assume that they recognize this fact. Be sure to stress the value of the whole of your offering. Don't assume that some valuable aspect of your offering that has not been identified as key by your customer has no value to them. Build a clear vision of the value of your offering in your customer's mind before getting into price negotiations.

If you find that you must give a price concession, seek something in return, and offer upfront no more than 75 percent of any concession you are prepared to make. Then hold firm. If the prospect detects any weakness in your resolve, they will continue the pressure for downward negotiations in price. Professional purchasers will return to previously closed aspects of the deal to try to shave off a little more advantage for themselves—only to return to the price issue again later. Waver, and you and your deal will die the slow and painful "death of a thousand cuts." Use what you've held back when you are certain that it will secure the business for you.

Even when the dealing is effectively finished, negotiations can still drag on unless you make a concerted effort to close. Human nature is such that the value we place on anything is often inversely proportional to its free availability, so use this fact to formulate effective final closing plays:

> Human nature is such that the value we place upon things is often inversely proportional to their free availability—use this knowledge in your closes.

- "Prices will go up shortly, but for a commitment now I may be able to fix prices at this level for the lifetime of this deal...."

- "I'd have to get Board approval for this level of discount, but if I could...."

Final negotiations are never easy, but if you plan, slow things down, anticipate ambushes, strategize on price, and close on scarcity, you'll sail cleanly over that final hurdle every time.

"The hero is no braver than an ordinary man, but he is brave five minutes longer."

RALPH WALDO EMERSON

Strategy 39

Once Beaten, Twice Smart

Once Beaten, Twice Smart

Turn Today's Losses into Tomorrow's Wins

Achieving a consistent 70 percent hit rate with the sales you pursue would probably keep you quite happy. Yet a 70 percent hit rate means losing almost half as many sales as you win. Most would accept these losses as the price paid for the wins they value so much, and write them off.

But what about the investment of time and effort in those lost sales? The challenge is to turn short-term failures into longer-term successes, to get some return on the investment of time, effort and resources. If you can achieve this, losses become part of winning, contributing towards your goal of winning an ever-greater share of the business you target. The single most effective tool for exploiting losses is the "De-brief" meeting.

De-briefing is not rocket science. All it amounts to is asking customers why you lost their business—and using that information to reduce the possibility that you might lose that way again. Even so, most sellers, even the better ones, do not employ any sort of De-brief mechanism—some because they don't want to dwell on the negative aspects of a loss, and some because they don't feel entitled to ask the customer for such feedback. If, however, you make it a goal to improve on the basis of lessons learned from lost business, De-briefs are positive experiences.

Think about it: you invested your time, effort and resources in trying to solve your customer's problem. The least the customer can do is help you to solve your problem now—your problem being that you need to improve what you do so that a similar loss is unlikely to happen again. You are entitled to a De-brief. Ask for one, every time.

A Personal Story from Bud Haney

Early in my selling career, I hit upon a strategy that helped me learn from every sales opportunity. Whenever I felt I had done my best and had presented an attractive proposition to a prospect, but did not leave with a sale, I did a follow-up interview the next day from my office. In order to keep the interview structured and not miss anything important, I worked from a written script and list of questions.

- "Mr. Smith, this is Bud Haney and I'm calling to thank you for the courtesy extended to me yesterday. I appreciate the opportunity to meet with you. As you could probably tell, I'm fairly new at selling, but I'm determined to make it my profession, and you could help me if you would be so kind. May I ask you a few questions?"

I have found that many people in business are eager to help younger people to develop their skills and will offer advice and encouragement if asked. These are some of the questions I asked when given the opportunity:

- "I did my best to convince you to buy from me yesterday, but you didn't. Could you tell me why?"

- "My appearance is very important to me. Was there anything about the way I was dressed or groomed that I could improve upon?"

287

- "Did you feel that I had a good grasp of your situation, enabling me to understand your company's needs?"

- "Did I approach you and treat you with the courtesy you expect?"

- "Was I able to answer your questions adequately?

- "Were there any holes in my presentation? Did you sense there were things I could have said—but didn't—that would have made my presentation more persuasive?"

- "When I call on you again, what do I have to do to get an order from you?"

I learned a lot from interviewing people who did not buy from me, and it helped me to sharpen my presentation and improve my selling technique. Incidentally, when I did have opportunity to call on these people again, they often gave me orders.

Besides the obvious benefits of offering you an insight into the reasons why you may have lost the business, a Debrief ironically also offers you the opportunity to develop your relationships within the lost account—something that will be extremely useful should you decide to continue your efforts with them. Many people do not like to disappoint, and some customer contacts may even feel bad about not giving you their business despite your hard work and professionalism. This can be a great opportunity to develop closer relationships with account contacts.

Running a De-brief

Keep your De-brief meeting short, focused, to-the-point and professional. You want the reasons why you did not win the business, pure and simple. Have a number of questions ready and take copious notes. At a very minimum, include the following:

Many people do not like to disappoint, and some customer contacts will feel bad about not awarding you business after a professional effort—this is a relationship-development opportunity.

- Can you detail the particular factors that prompted you to select another vendor?

- If these factors had been present in our proposal, would you have been prepared to do business with us? If not, why not?

- How else would you suggest that we might have improved our chances of winning your business?

- Would you be prepared to give us copies of non-proprietary parts of the successful vendor's proposal to allow us to analyze more closely why their bid was more successful, helping us to address any shortcomings in our approach to winning future business with your organization? (Don't be shy about asking for this sort of material— many customers will provide this valuable input for your competitive analysis.)

- Are you prepared to consider us for future business? If not, why not?

- Are there any other current requirements we might be able to help you with?

- Can we stay in touch with you to keep you informed of developments with our company and offerings?

You will find that even the very general questions above will drive the meeting sufficiently to allow you to build a good understanding of why you were unsuccessful.

One of the keys to a successful De-brief is attitude. If you feel too disappointed to follow the general guidelines below, you might do well to forget the idea of a De-brief altogether—you might do more harm than good. So:

- Be pleasant.

- Hold your head high.

- Be the consummate professional.

- Take charge of the De-brief.

- Be careful not to come across as aggressive, bitter or defensive (Disappointed is OK!)

- Pursue discussion of the reasons for your loss until you have a clear understanding.

- Be positive. Remember you would like to do future business with these people.

- Don't be argumentative—stay away from unnecessary detail of any contentious aspects of the prospect's handling of the evaluation process.

- Don't be over-friendly—don't crawl.

- Don't allow the conversation to move away from the job at hand to easier general chit-chat until you have the answers for which you came.

Remember, you lost the sale, so don't try to resell. Just get the information you need to ensure that you win next time.

Using the Outcome of Your De-brief

A De-brief is only as useful as the use to which you put what you learn. Be sure to:

1. Share these results with anyone who had input into the unsuccessful proposal or relationship, and with anyone who may have input into any future sales, particularly in the same account.

2. Brainstorm with your team on how best to address these shortcomings in the future.

3. Put a formal plan in place to address any problem areas.

Lost sales are the clearest signal that you may be doing something wrong. Problem is, you don't usually know just how wrong until it's too late—until you've invested a large amount of time and effort. Don't just accept losses. Ask for a De-brief to question everyone—using anything useful you uncover to reduce the chances that it might happen again.

Remember: Once beaten, twice smart.

"The greatest test of courage on earth is to bear defeat without losing heart."
ROBERT G. INGERSOLL

Strategy 40

"I Hate Writing Business Proposals"

"I Hate Writing Business Proposals"

...Doesn't Mean I Can't Write Winners

Potential purchasers have more options than ever before. Most of them are so closely matched in terms of product/ service performance, quality and price that it is becoming ever more difficult for purchasers to choose between suppliers. They now routinely call for potential suppliers to prepare proposals for every acquisition that they make, large or small.

If you can't write good proposals, life is going to become more and more difficult for you!

One vital element in improving the quality of your proposals is a compelling framework—a structure for your proposal that sells your ideas and solutions. This strategy introduces the winning proposal framework—a structure to maximize the success of every future proposal that you write.

Let's Talk Proposals

If, instead of writing a proposal, you were having a one-on-one conversation with your customer, trying to sell your superior solution to his or her requirements, you would very likely make the points outlined in this greatly condensed conversation:

"...we understand your requirements thoroughly...we have a solution to those requirements...this is why our solution is so good for you...here are the costs for our proposed solution...yes, we can prove every claim we've made...."

Effective business proposals establish this dialogue with their readers, and that's why we've included each of the above elements in our structure for writing winning proposals.

"We Understand Your Requirements Thoroughly"

The first thing you absolutely must establish is that you understand the customer's requirements inside out—you have as detailed an appreciation of what the customer is trying to achieve as he or she does (perhaps even better). Many proposal-writers undervalue the persuasive power of re-stating their understanding of the customer's requirements —doing an exemplary job of outlining the requirements in your proposals can very often be the difference between winning and losing the target business. Dale Carnegie said that sales success depends upon *"getting them saying 'Yes, Yes' immediately."* How better to do so than confirm the requirements they outlined to you?

The logical first section in your proposal should, therefore, detail the customer requirements, and for discussion purposes we will call this section: **The Requirement**.

> The most effective business proposals establish an easy dialogue with their readers— drawing the readers in.

"We Have a Solution to the Requirement"

Your first section sets out to convince your customer that you understand what he's trying to achieve. You now have his attention, so continue your conversation by describing how you can address the customer's requirements—outline your solution. This is the pivotal section of your proposal. You are, after all, writing the proposal to sell this solution.

The second section of your proposal should be called **The Proposed Solution**.

"This is Why Our Solution is So Good for You"

The customer will certainly want to know just what *is* your solution—what benefits will accrue if they select your solution over your competitor's.

You must emphasize the particular strengths of your solution, and minimize any weaknesses. At the same time, highlight any weaknesses in likely competitors' solutions, and minimize the importance of any strengths they might be able to demonstrate. This is your third proposal section: **Benefits of the Proposed Solution**.

> You must emphasize the particular strengths of your offering.

"Here are the Costs Associated with our Solution"

Now that you have established that you understand the requirement, that you have a good solution to these requirements, and that your solution will be of particular benefit to your customer, your customer is certainly going to want to know how much this "best of all possible solutions" is going to cost.

Your fourth section will detail the costs associated with your proposed solution, Call it: **Costs**.

"We Can Prove All of the Claims Made in this Proposal"

Up to this point, you have focused on communicating one basic message—*"We have the best possible solution to your requirements."* To communicate this message effectively, you should confine yourself to the main points supporting this contention, staying away from excessive detail that might distract the customer, drawing her attention off on a tangent.

In each of the sections mentioned above, include only as much detail as necessary to support the message you are trying to communicate. All of the detailed technical material —technical specifications, product descriptions, supporting research, and so on—should be confined to appendices at the back of your proposal, with your main text making frequent reference to the presence of this supporting material in the **Appendices** section of your proposal.

The Winning Framework for Your Proposals

By establishing this simple *Requirements–Solution– Benefits–Costs–Appendices* dialogue with your customer in your proposals, you end up with a basic framework for all of your proposals.

The figure below graphically illustrates this basic proposal model. Besides the self-explanatory *Title Page & Table of*

Contents, this figure also contains an additional section —the **Executive Summary**.

WINNING PROPOSAL STRUCTURE

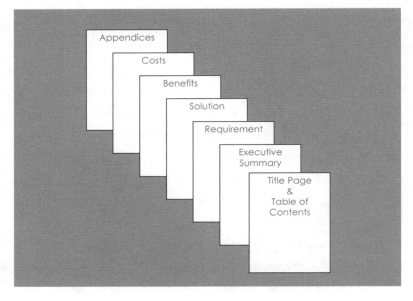

Executive Summary

The **Executive Summary** section provides an overview of the total content of your proposal. It is designed for those senior executives in your customer organization who do not have time to review any more than the highlights of your proposal. It is also designed to be a general introduction for other readers who wish to read your proposal in its entirety, orienting them on how your proposal is laid out and preparing them for the main points of your proposal.

Think of your **Executive Summary** as the equivalent of a book cover—a quick-to-read summary that provides readers with what they need to "buy your story." Build your **Executive Summary** using the winning structure—with a few lines summarizing each of your completed main sections. After the **Solution** section, the **Executive Summary** is arguably the most important section of any proposal—it may well be the only section that some decision-makers will bother to read. Invest time to get it right.

Adapt and Thrive

Undoubtedly, some of your proposals will not be of a size that allows you to make your case adequately in six sections. Similarly, some of your proposals will not be longer than a single letter. This does not, however, prevent you from using the basic *Executive Summary–Requirements–Solution–Benefits–Costs–Appendices* structure.

A one-page proposal letter should still use the same structure, with brief paragraphs substituting for the sections discussed above. Similarly, larger proposals may demand many more sections, with entirely different titles. The key is to ensure that, however large or small your proposal, you successfully establish this dialogue flow—get your readers saying, "yes, yes," throughout.

We can't promise that adopting this structure will result in a love for writing proposals—but we can guarantee that you'll get a vastly higher hit rate for your hateful labors.

> *"There is nothing to writing. All you do is sit down at a typewriter and open a vein."*
> RED SMITH